That Part!

THAT PART!

WHAT SOME KNOW
BUT WON'T TELL YOU ABOUT
MOTHERHOOD

BY

DIONNE JOYNER-WEEMS

That Part!: What Some Know but Won't Tell You about Motherhood
© 2023 Dionne Joyner-Weems

Published by Audacity Group LLC.
DionneJoynerWeems.com
Baltimore, Maryland.

Paperback: 979-8-9893290-0-7
Hardcover: 979-8-9893290-3-8
Ebook: 979-8-9893290-1-4
Audiobook: 979-8-9893290-2-1

Cover design and illustrations by Audacity Group LLC
Interior design by Liz Schreiter
Edited and produced by Reading List Editorial
ReadingListEditorial.com

This book is dedicated to my three sons, Shawn, Liam, and Emery. I love you to the moon and back, though you constantly tell me, "That's not that far."

CONTENTS

WHAT DO I KNOW?

When I was pregnant with my first child in 2010, I purchased every childbirth book imaginable, from *What to Expect When You're Expecting* and *The Womanly Art of Breastfeeding* to *The Happiest Baby on the Block* and *Baby 411*. Two years later, when we found out we were expecting twins, I purchased double the books, along with every edition of the Holy Bible. I think I may have even thrown in a Quran or two for flavoring, and I'm not even Muslim. I just knew that with the new challenge of raising three boys under the age of three, I needed to know that God, Buddha, Yahweh, Jehovah, Allah, Shiva, and the artist formerly known as Prince were listening.

A little background: I'm a classic type-A personality, an Aries sun sign with a Sagittarius rising. I'm an eighties baby, born and raised on the west side of Baltimore—my hometown and my heart. Just imagine a wiry (ninety pounds when wet) Black girl, bobbing and weaving through Sandtown-Winchester. My neighborhood shaped me within a redlined community that framed the way I saw the world. A concoction of grit and a dash of grace, I'm the firstborn child and a manic overthinker who has the nerve to be stubborn. I'm Zoloft's wet dream. I don't want to get things done simply; I want to get things done perfectly. So, it would only be natural that I would approach childbirth and parenting as a DIY project that I could research and perfect.

Of the twenty-seven books I purchased in preparation for my sons' arrival, do you know how many I referenced after we brought our babies home? That's right: zero, zilch, nada. Well, we did use two books to balance the changing table we purchased from Ikea—but there was no reading involved. This is not because they served their purpose and told me everything I needed to know. It was because the authors approached motherhood as doctors, nurses, or teachers. Their eye was fixed with a scientific lens, not based on lived experience. And let me tell you, you need lived experience when it's three o'clock in the morning and your breasts are engorged. Your mood swings are tangled in knotted chains. You haven't eaten or slept longer than twenty minutes over the course of seventy-two hours. And your baby or babies' blood-curdling shrills are sending chills down your spine. At that moment, you do not need a doctor to reinforce the swaddling method. At that moment, you need someone to tell you, "It's okay that you want to scream. You are not the first person to think about hurling your baby to Pluto. It's okay that you feel like happiness is just outside your reach and you are second-guessing your decision or ability to be a mother. You are not a horrible person for not feeling that intimate connection with your child that everyone raves about." You need someone to say, "It's okay. I can relate."

Well, I don't have a PhD in counseling. But I do have lots of experience being a mother who has crawled through the darkest valley. From the fear of raising little Black boys in America to trying to establish boundaries or battling the shame of depression while navigating the sudden change in personal relationships, I made it to the other side.

Everyone told me how fast time would fly, but no one told me the deeper reason for savoring those moments. As soon as we laid eyes on our firstborn son on Wednesday, August, 24, 2011, Shawn (who we called S. Dot affectionately) changed my life. Every experience I had as a mother pulled back the curtain on how I saw the world and who I wanted to be as a woman. The first five years of motherhood were a sobering test of self-reflection. And I chronicled my epiphanies and ah-ha moments in my diary daily, and I continued to write my reflections for the five years that followed. I had always loved storytelling, but motherhood reignited my passion. All of West Baltimore came out of me. I was raw and uncut, you hear me? I wrote what I saw as I felt it!

Becoming a mother is powerful, but it can also be isolating. It's unfiltered madness that is enlightening, exhausting, and affirming. More mothers should be encouraged to share the blessings in the lessons. Even after more than twelve years, my life has changed and my children are older, but it was those first precious five years of raising three boys under three that I not only discovered my voice but also embraced my womanhood.

DELIVERY FIGHT CLUB

Before delivering my son, S. Dot, I asked every mother I knew, "How does childbirth feel?" The clearest answer I received was, "Imagine your worst menstrual cramps, and multiply that times 100." Let's just say that did not nearly detail what I felt. But my girlfriend/hair stylist, Jennifer, who has an eleven-year-old and a thirteen-year-old, told me a woman is not supposed to tell a new mother what delivering a child feels like, so as to avoid scaring her. I guess it's like the first rule of Fight Club. You do not talk about Fight Club.

Well, since I'm all about sharing, I would like to offer a few personal tips.

1. Don't prolong the pain of contractions by staying in the bed. Get up and walk! And when you don't feel like walking, or you think you can't . . . walk some more!

2. Prepare a bag of snacks for whoever is going to be in the delivery room with you. You may be in for a long stretch. I was in labor for sixteen hours, and things can turn on a dime. There is no time for people to be running back and forth to the hospital cafeteria. A father gave me this tip a week before I had S. Dot. It was beyond helpful.

3. Having a mirror is cool. When you are pushing, it can increase your sense of control because you're able to see what is happening. I had one, but I didn't look at it because my eyes were squeezed tight, as an awkwardly shaped gooey bowling ball propelled out of my very small vagina. I didn't need that reflected back at me.

4. It's a great idea for your birthing partner to wear tennis shoes, but not a good idea for them to wear *new* tennis shoes. My husband is still complaining about afterbirth spilling on his new Adidas Sambas. PS: That same father from #2 gave me this advice. His children are now eleven and seventeen, so there must be some things men never forget.

WARNING:

Do not read any further if you are the type to overthink or make things worse than they are.

I see you're going to read on anyway. We are so alike.

Please remember to breathe! It sounds simple, but if you think about it, what is the first thing that happens to you when your body is hit with pain? Your body tightens. You focus so much on the source of the pain that your breathing becomes shallow.

Body: What in God's name was that?

Breathing: I don't know, but I'm not going anywhere until we find out what is going on and how do we make it stop!

I'm serious: concentrate on your breathing, not on the pain. I'm not talking about that theatrical "He, he, he, whoo! He, he, he, whoo!" Save that for the silver screen. When I say breathe, I mean those deep yoga breaths. Scoff if you must! I swear when I was hit with a contraction, I would actually take a deep breath as I pushed out my stomach, and as I exhaled I brought my stomach in. Realistically, you have a baby inside of you, so you haven't been able to voluntarily hold in your stomach for months, but whatever little in and out movements you can visualize your stomach doing will help.

Here is my last little tidbit: I was in labor without an epidural for sixteen hours. (More on this in "The Natural Birth Dare.") When it was time to push out S. Dot, my body was ready. I was so sick of dealing with the pain of the contractions, my body welcomed the urge to push. It was like finding water in the desert. As a matter of fact, the doctors tried to stop me from pushing because they questioned whether it was really time. I made it crystal clear: "I am not telling you that I THINK I have to push, I am telling you I AM PUSHING!"

I know this may sound crazy, but pushing did not hurt. It just required a lot of effort, and because I was so happy to not feel those horrible, tongue-trembling, mouth-quivering contractions, I was more than willing to push with all the effort I had. Just when I thought I was in the home stretch, I pushed down hard, and my son's head started to crown, but out of nowhere, I felt a searing, blistering pain in my nether regions.

If I had to describe it, I would compare it to what I've always imagined Harry Potter's scar feels like when Voldemort is close. If that reference meant absolutely nothing to you, let's just say it hurt extremely bad and I stopped pushing. My doctor looked me in the eyes and said, "What you feel is the Ring of Fire, but if you can just push through it, I promise it will be over in a second." Pardon me? You want me to push through a Ring of Fire!?! Who am I, Johnny Cash?

Because I had sampled the pain that would soon greet me when I bore down, I wasn't eager to give that final push. But I knew the longer I avoided it, the more likely it would be that all the effort I'd made to push my son this far down would be for nothing. If I couldn't get S. Dot out, I would have to have a C-section, which I was trying desperately to avoid.

Time stood still. I went silent. I ignored everyone in the room and began reasoning with myself. I closed my eyes, and I swear I saw Jesus. My hand on the Bible! People often laugh when I say this, and ask,

"What did Jesus look like?" I'd say it was more of a feeling. I was surrounded by darkness, and then stars appeared. Next, there was a guttural scream—which I'm pretty sure was me and not Jesus. After two pushes, our son was here.

In life, sometimes you have to push through the pain . . . literally.

THE NATURAL BIRTH DARE

I delivered our son after sixteen hours of labor without medication. Up until the last push, the nurses told us that our hospital room was one of the quietest they had ever witnessed. Why? Because it took all of my concentration to focus on what was happening to me. Now, before I continue, do you remember that obnoxious kid in grade school whose eyes got a little wider when they were faced with the treacherous "double dare"? Yeah, I was that child. Anyone who knows me will tell you that I have an incessant need to prove myself. It's a horrible trait, and I'm working on it.

In my second trimester, my husband and I were leaving my uncle's house, and someone asked, "Are you going to deliver the baby naturally?" Before I could even answer, everyone was already laughing at the thought of me denying medication. In my head, they might as well have double dared me.

My husband loves me and hates to see me in any pain. He encouraged me to drop my idea of a natural birth. But the more he questioned me, the more indignant I became. One day I was so drunk off my defiance that we had a conversation that went like this:

> **Him:** Baby, everyone knows how strong you are. When the time comes, just take the epidural.
>
> **Me:** Years ago, my ancestors, slaves, would trudge through the cotton field literally barefoot and pregnant, and as the pain of giving birth struck their bodies, do you know what they would do?

Him: <side eye> I don't like where this is going, but I am sure you are still going to tell me . . .

Me: <ignoring his sarcasm> They would squat where they stood—

Him: <interrupting> Are we sure they squatted, or was it more of a kneel?

Me: <ignoring his sarcasm . . . again> THEY WOULD *SQUAT*—

Him: <interrupting . . . again> Hold on! You weren't there. What makes you think they didn't kneel?

Me: FINE!!! <now shouting> THEY WOULD KNEEL IN THE SPOT THEY ONCE STOOD IN, AND WITH ALL THE POWER IN THEIR BODY— DESIGNED BY GOD TO CARRY AND GIVE LIFE—THEY WOULD BITE DOWN ON A STICK AND PUSH OUT THE BABY, PRAY OVER THEM, STAND UP, AND CONTINUE PICKING COTTON. DO YOU UNDERSTAND WHAT I'M SAYING?

Him: <pause> Baby, you're not a slave, and sticks aren't covered under our insurance.

Such the funny guy! Here's the real point: after being blessed to deliver a healthy, 6 lb. 12.2-ounce beautiful baby boy (nineteen inches long), I realized that no matter how you deliver a child—whether naturally, with an epidural, via C-section, or with a stick— the fact that your child is here makes you a HERO.

It's childbirth, not a competition. Everyone wins.

I DON'T KNOW HOW TO RAISE A CHILD

When I was pregnant with S. Dot, I remember sharing my nervousness with my father. I didn't grow up dreaming of having children. And because of a few of my "less than desirable" character traits (e.g., all those associated with being a type-A personality and a typical Aries), I just knew I would drive my son into the hands of a therapist.

While I'm considered a bit of a perfectionist, on the outside, my husband is viewed as the calm one. He has the greatest sense of humor and the most ingenious mind, but don't let the smooth exterior fool you; he's a bit of a nut himself. Together we make for a great reality show, but how would we fare as parents?

I called my father one day and said, "Daddy, what am I going to do? Raising a daughter is one thing, but raising a boy comes with a different set of responsibilities. The world is rough on young men, especially Black men. There are so many pitfalls to avoid, and the odds are stacked against them. I want S. Dot to be strong but not insensitive. He needs to value education, but I want him to appreciate the arts and creativity. He needs to be a fighter without being a bully. I want him to respect others but never allow himself to be blinded. He needs to know the importance of giving and sharing, but he can't be a pushover. He has to stand his ground, but I need him to recognize when it's best to walk away. I want him to be a serious man but still be able to laugh at himself . . . Daddy, I want my son to be a good person."

My father responded, "Just continue to be the person that *you* are, and the rest will happen."

That's the way my father is. I come to him with what seems to me to be a complex issue, and his solution is simple. Children want to be what they see. They want to do what you do. So, if you're a parent doing interesting things and being a good person, your child will do the same.

> My child will be the best that he can be, but it starts with me.

MY BABY STORY

Are These Contractions or Braxton Hicks?

Now that my son is a year and a half, I've been in a reflective mood.

If you are from the East Coast and you gave birth on August 24, 2011, then our stories start off very similarly. My son S. Dot was born the day after the East Coast's first major earthquake and the day before Hurricane Irene.

On August 24, I woke up in the middle of the night and felt stomach cramps but couldn't distinguish whether these were the usual Braxton Hicks I had been experiencing for a few weeks or real contractions. Here I was at one o'clock in the morning actually googling "What do contractions feel like?" Keep in mind, I took childbirth classes and read every book known to man, yet here I was at the Mac altar praying to the Google gods to diagnose me.

The cramps were getting worse, and my stomach felt as hard as a boulder, but where before it would subside and become soft again, that wasn't happening this time. I tried to lie back down because, if I *was* having contractions, my goal was to stay at home as long as possible. I had never been admitted to a hospital, and I really wanted to stay in the comfort of my own home. So, instead of calling the doctor, I waddled back to bed and tried to sleep it off. Yes, you heard me. I tried to sleep off the fact that a human being was trying to propel from my body.

I tossed and turned, which for some reason did not alarm or wake my husband. To be fair, after I hit my fifth month of pregnancy, sleeping on my back or stomach went out the window, and trailing behind it went any chance of a comfortable night's sleep, so my husband was pretty used to sleeping next to a breakdancing baby walrus (I'm playing the baby walrus in this scene). After half an hour, I couldn't lie in the bed any longer.

I remembered that warm showers help to soothe contractions, so I went into the bathroom. But before I could turn on the shower, a series of disgusting things happened. First, let me preface this by saying that when I learned that the body tries to purge itself before delivering a baby, I didn't take it literally. At two a.m., as I stood in my bathroom, it felt as if I was going to implode.

I was confused: my body was telling me I had to have a bowel movement and throw up at the same time. It was acting as if the police had just shown up at the door and it had ten seconds to flush the drugs and hide the money. It was every man for himself. I was deliriously dizzy, but get this: I was still determined to ride it out. Yes, I told myself, when the bathroom stops spinning, I'm going to hop into the shower and then get back into the bed. Luckily, God knows I'm hard-headed, so He showed me the one thing I would respond to: my mucus plug broke and I started bleeding. EUREKA! (Shout out to *The Backyardigans*. It's like *Wu-Tang Forever*.)

As I turned to get my husband out of my bed, my knees buckled under the weight of a massive contraction, and I fell to the bathroom floor. The last thought that ran through my head as my husband gassed his little Hyundai Sonata was, *I hope I didn't get blood on the bathroom rug. We just bought it.*

Contractions are the Devil.

THE ROSE THAT GREW FROM CONCRETE

I'd just left the office to grab some lunch from one of the many food trucks downtown. As I was walking up the street, I heard a woman shouting, "If you don't move your f@#king ass. Sh#t! Let me have to tell your dumb ass again, and I'm going to beat ya little ass!" At that moment, I turned to see a "young lady" (please note the quotation marks) in her late twenties pulling the arm of a roughly five-year-old girl who was, obviously, walking too slowly for her mother. Honestly, I was praying that at any second, a lightning bolt would scorch the afternoon sky and the woman would explode where she stood, leaving only the soles of her fake Ugg boots melted on the sidewalk.

I couldn't control my disgust, and judging by the look on the mother's face, she had noticed. But staying true to her character (ignorant woman with no home training), she coiled her neck in rage and mumbled, "You need to mind your f@cking business," then she snatched her daughter by the shoulder of her coat and marched her across the street. I felt heat race through my body. Any rational human being without children could see this was wrong, but now that I have a child, my need to protect is near primal. I wanted to hold the little girl close and tell her how beautiful and smart she is, how no one has the right to hurt her with their words . . . I wanted to tell her that everything is going to be okay. But is it?

I can't be the only person who has a story like this. More and more, I see parents treating their children like stray dogs, and it's heartbreaking. And if they aren't treating their babies like afterthoughts, they're treating each other with no regard. I can drive through my city at any time of the day and find at least one guy looking like Lord knows what, smoking a blunt with his toddler at his heels, or find a woman on her cell talking about everything but while her daughter is sitting close by listening.

Do you know the reason I don't like Whitney Houston's "Greatest Love of All"? It's because I've seen enough of these children to make me question if we are all trying to get to the same future.

How can we expect children to do better if they don't know better?

Yet, when I'm discouraged, I am reminded that as long as we believe there is a power greater than ourselves, nothing against us will prosper. And for every parent who makes me hang my head and weep, there are parents like those I've met throughout my pregnancy who make me hold my head high and smile.

Children are resilient beings, and they are influenced by everything around them. They are able to see past the darkness and imagine something better. With this understanding, I am going to continue to pray and focus on being a good parent to my little boy—and hope that I can elevate those around me by example.

Long live the rose that grew
from the concrete when no
one else ever cared.

—Tupac Shakur

LIFE IS ONE FREAKING TEST

No matter how much you plan, the unexpected will happen. You lay your clothes out for work the night before just to spend an hour the next morning trying to find your bra. Before leaving the house, you save an address in your phone's GPS just to spend the next hour lost, in the car, trying to locate a signal. You pick out the perfect outfit for your son, rush him to his first preschool open-house, and as soon as you park he throws up all over his clothes and car seat. It never freaking fails!

It's like one of my favorite Alanis Morrissette songs, "Ironic."

And I am discovering that irony is no clearer than when you have children. Personally, I pride myself on being a good planner, but there is no amount of planning that a child cannot undo. I love my S. Dot, but his timing sucks! I swear, sometimes I think he's doing it on purpose. All day, my son will run and play around the house, and ten minutes before my family or friends come over to see him—"CRASH"! Somehow this little boy trips over the same rug he has been running over ALL DAY. He lands facedown on the hardwood floor, his lip is bleeding, and he has a knot the size of a plum in the center of his forehead. The doorbell rings, and people enter the house to the sound of a screaming child, blood pouring from his mouth.

I am convinced that children are living, walking, breathing emergency drills. They help parents learn to act fast on their feet and stay fluid. I am not where I want to be, but I am a hell of a lot more flexible than I used to be, and that is thanks to my son, "The Emergency Drill!"

BEEEEEP!
This is only a test.
BEEEEEP! If this had
been an actual emegency,
there would be no
broadcast station to
help us!

HELLO BREASTFEEDING

I Gave You Three Months

I was adamant that I was going to breastfeed my son exclusively for the first 365 days of his life. I read every book you could imagine— *Breastfeeding Made Simple: Seven Natural Laws for Nursing Mothers, The Womanly Art of Breastfeeding, The Breastfeeding Book: Everything You Need to Know about Nursing Your Child from Birth through Weaning*, and the list goes on. And let's not discuss the amount of online video clips I watched. Every time my husband walked past me on the computer, there was a titty on the screen.

In my mind, there were *no* other options. Breast milk is what my baby needed, so breast milk was what my baby was going to get. When people offered me other suggestions, I would tune them out. Deep down I knew they were trying to help, but I took their comments as being negative or doubting my abilities.

Lucky for me, my son latched on immediately after delivery. I had a great lactation specialist who was very supportive, and even when I returned home, I could send her an email or give her a call on the breastfeeding hotline. (Yes, there's a hotline.)

For the first couple of days, my body was still reeling from childbirth. Though S. Dot was feeding, my whole state of mind was numb. Honestly, I couldn't tell you if I was using the "proper" breastfeeding techniques. I just knew my son was eating, and that was all that mattered to me. Until two weeks later. All I can remember is that things got real raw, real painful, REAL FREAKING FAST! I look at that period as my first bout of foolish selflessness. See, as long as my son was feeding and seemed comfortable, I wouldn't move him—no matter how badly my nipples blistered or how uncomfortable I felt. I know, not my smartest moment. But in my defense, my hormones were monstrous. I couldn't think straight.

After a few tips from the lactation specialist and a *lot* of lanolin ointment, I am happy to say that I started to feel much better.

When it comes to breastfeeding, you can meet ten women, and they will give you ten different perspectives. For me, I believe it starts with a good support group. It helps when you are surrounded by people with experience. Personally, my mother breastfed me for two weeks, then she stopped because "It felt creepy" (her words, not mine). My aunt wanted to breastfeed, but her children didn't take to the process. I had girlfriends, but most did not have children. My husband was supportive, but he wasn't as hell-bent on S. Dot being breastfed as I was. Between you and me, I think his mentality was, "If he doesn't want your breasts, I'll take them!"

I had to push myself and figured out a lot on my own.

After three weeks, my husband would bottle feed S. Dot once at night to give me an opportunity to sleep. After six weeks, we would give him one bottle of breast milk in the afternoon and one during those early morning "God what time is it?" feedings. This offered me a much-needed break, it provided my husband and son bonding time, and it introduced S. Dot to the bottle, which was helpful when he was being watched by family members. Everything seemed to be working. I was even pumping and storing my milk in the freezer. I felt like a well-oiled milking machine.

And just when I thought I had the hang of things, I hit a wall . . . HARD!

S. Dot was around two months old, and he was eating every two to two and a half hours (nonstop). It was beginning to take a toll on me. Every time I would breastfeed, the sensation felt like Freddy Krueger dragging his long metal nails along the width of a chalkboard. When he would suckle, it was sensory overload. I would look at him through grit teeth, resisting the urge to yank him off my chest. My brain could not process all of the feelings. I know I sound horrible, but that's what you see when you read my diary.

There were some feedings where I was counting down the seconds to get that boy off my chest. After twenty minutes, I would look down at him, and he would actually be asleep, using me like some common pacifier. I began dreading breastfeeding. I felt SOOOOO uncomfortable. My poor husband would try to carry a conversation with me while I was nursing, and I would imagine lasers shooting from my eyes and his head rolling across the bedroom floor. When I say I hit the wall, I mean I went through those bricks headfirst.

By the time I came to the end of three months, I couldn't take it anymore. Based on my earlier experience, I could now see that I was bordering again on the edge of foolish selflessness. I felt like I failed, and the guilt was heavy. Then, it hit me: *I love my son, and I want to enjoy the last days of my maternity leave relishing his light, not imagining hurling him across the room followed by his father's laser-seared head.* So, I stopped breastfeeding at three months and opted to pump my milk exclusively.

If Mommy isn't comfortable, no one is comfortable.

GUN CONTROL–JUST HEAR ME OUT!

If I had heard the news regarding Sandy Hook Elementary School sixteen months ago, before the birth of my son, I am sure I would have been horrified that something so vile could happen to innocent people. But last month, as my son lay in his crib for his afternoon nap, news surfaced that a man had taken the lives of twenty children and killed six teachers who died protecting them, and my breath became shallow, my heart raced, my knees buckled, heat rose through my body, my eyes welled with tears, and I instantly felt nauseous. I didn't move. I was numb. Before my son, I knew love, but after his birth, I understood love, and the thought of losing him penetrates the core of my being.

That is why I don't understand the "debate" when it comes to gun control. Yes, the Second Amendment states that citizens have the right to bear arms, which I have no issue with. But please keep in mind that the Constitution was written in 1787. People had muskets, which took forever to load and fired one pellet at a time. Cannons were far from portable, and three-pound cannonballs aren't artillery pieces you just shoot willy-nilly. There is a stark difference when you compare citizens of the 1700s to those civilians in 2013 who feel the need to carry rapid-fire semi-automatic rifles that come with magazine clips that hold ten rounds of ammunition. I think if Thomas Jefferson were around today, his Facebook status would be "WTF!"

<Deep inhale> I am not saying that responsible adults should lose their right to own guns, and I am not proclaiming to have some grand solution, but I do know this: a compromise is necessary, restrictions are

needed, the government will never take the place of parents loving and nurturing their children, education and the arts should be supported throughout all cities and communities, and mental health and wellness should be vigorously pursued with treatment readily available for anyone in need. <Out of breath>

It is imperative that a systematic change occur in our society, if not for our sake, then for the sake of our children.

There is a phrase that comes to mind for me whenever I hear about tragedies like Sandy Hook or countless other stories of victims of violence across the United States: "There but for the grace of God go I."

We must protect our children with the same energy used to protect guns.

WHAT'S A WEEKEND TO A BABY?

Babies could give a damn about three-day weekends, or any weekend for that matter. Do you know why? Because babies are survivalists. Before S. Dot came along, my husband and I lived for the weekends. They were our holy grail . . . damn near sacred!

We went to bed late and woke up even later. You try calling us at noon on a Saturday, and best believe you're getting the voice-mail. We went out to eat, we took naps, we drank wine, we engaged in "adult activities" (which got us into this predicament), and we spent hours on the couch in front of the TV, watching *Grey's Anatomy*, trying to figure out what was going to happen next with Meredith and Derek. As Bernie Mac would say, "Good living! Good living!"

My, how the mighty have fallen. Having a child changes *everything*. No, not some things . . . EVERYTHING. I love my little man, but why is his internal clock stuck on six a.m. as his wake-up time?!? He doesn't have a job or any previous commitments. Is he known for running late, so to overcompensate he gets up entirely too early?

And I'm not complaining because it's Saturday and my husband and I have worked hard all week, or because I have cramps and my head hurts. It's the fact that it's six a.m., we're standing over this crib half-alive, and this kid is acting as if he's a presidential candidate before his first pep rally . . . *revved up and ready to go!*

All I am saying is the next time I'm at work and a coworker without children tells me they had a nice weekend but it went by too quickly, I will refrain from kneeing them in their balls and/or lady parts, because I do not want to ruin their chance of having children . . . because therein lies the real payback.

Parenting is not for the faint of heart, or those fond of sleeping.

DREAM BIG

I woke up this morning with a thought: *Most dreams are strongest when you are experiencing them. Then, when you wake up, the memory feels real but a bit distant. And, as time passes, the details of the dream become a blur . . . yet the feeling always remains.*

Today marks the birthday of Dr. Martin Luther King Jr., as well as the second inauguration of our nation's first African American President, Barack Obama. During the president's first campaign, my son S. Dot wasn't even an idea. Yet, I did see how Barack Obama's run for office affected other children. Of course, for most children, the meaning behind Obama's historic rise had to be explained to them by adults. And it was then that it hit me.

This chapter in history carries a different footnote for each generation that reads it.

For my mother and father, they think of the trials their parents experienced while growing up.

My mother was born in Richmond, Virginia, one of the oldest and most historic places in the United States. Often, when people speak of the city, they reference Richmond's role in the American Revolution and Civil War, but for me, I just remember the strong smell of tobacco in the air when we would visit from Baltimore.

My father was born in Georgetown, South Carolina, in a little community called Dunbar. His people were a part of the Gullah culture in the Low Country region. We're talking dirt roads, tin roofs, sweetgrass baskets, heavy quilts, and soft water that would leave my body feeling oddly smoother and silkier after every wash. Even the language they spoke, a kind of creole, differed from the city talk I was used to.

I didn't realize it then, but though I grew up in Baltimore, my family was strongly influenced by a down south acumen and a strong sense of history, heritage, and community.

For my parents, when Obama was elected, they were seeing Dr. King's dream in action; for my grandparents, they think of the challenges they overcame to ensure the livelihood of their family. It was Dr. King's dream personified, and for people like my great-grandmother (who passed in October 2012 at the age of ninety-four), the election of Barack Obama made her feel that the harsh life she survived actually birthed purpose. It was Dr. King's dream "alive."

But today, as we roll around on the floor with our sixteen-month-old son playing and laughing, we are slowly sharing the details of a dream that was long since dreamt, but the feeling remains. When he is old enough, we will say, "Yes, the election and re-election of our nation's forty-fourth president was viewed as Dr. King's dream personified, in action and alive . . . but it is yet to be fulfilled."

As long as there are injustices in the world spurred by racism, you cannot say that Dr. King's dream has been realized, but we are blessed, "Black, white, Jews and Gentiles, Protestants and Catholics." We live in a time where we do not question whether our dreams are obtainable, because we have witnessed enough to truly believe that anything is possible. But we have so much further to go, I will raise my son to not be discouraged but aware, to not be clouded by hate but to understand the strength of love, and to never believe he is inferior, for he is the product of generations that have seen far worse and still prevailed.

> Allow history to make you better . . . not bitter.

I'M ALWAYS IN MY OWN WAY

I'm what a diplomatic person calls a "perfectionist" and what a person who loves me calls a "f-ing nut." I want everything to be just right. And guess how often that happens? Not often enough.

"It's like S. Dot knows . . ."

For example, I sat down this weekend with the intention to work on my blog during S. Dot's naps, and of course he decided to wake up early each time. It's as if he knows that Mommy has something she wants to do while he is sleeping, so let's have a massive poop and start shouting incoherently.

Then, last night, after putting S. Dot soundly to bed, I turned on the computer, ready to take over the world one click at a time . . . and the computer crashed. WTF! Nothing ever goes smoothly for me. After my husband finished the phone call with AppleCare (who didn't care), he saw me with my head in my hand, and I lost it!

"What am I going to do without a computer? I don't know what I'm doing! I have stories to write. I have edits to make! I have to make changes to this website! Does this site even make sense? Is it good? Who am I to talk about parenting? I know *nothing*! Do you think I'll offend someone? I most definitely will offend someone! What about S. Dot? What makes me think I have time for this? What's my point? What's my vision? What's the end goal? Do you think people will like it? Wait, where are you going?"

I started writing about my motherhood journey because I love talking about being a new parent, but then my ego, masquerading as "perfection," begins to cloud my judgment. Sometimes, I need to take a chill pill and breathe it out. I have an awful habit of getting in my own way. Do you remember when your mother would say, "You're too smart for your own good"? Well, that is truer of me today than it was when I was younger. So many people around me are progressing, and sometimes I think I have to follow a particular path— but that is far from true.

P.S. I guarantee this little topic will rear its head again.

I need to learn to bend before I break.

I HAVE TO STOP COMPARING MYSELF

I watched Beyoncé's beautiful documentary, *Life Is but a Dream* this weekend with my husband. Of course, I could have listened to her talk about motherhood for the full ninety minutes, but I'm a bit of a nut that way. As the end credits scrolled, I turned off the TV, brushed my teeth, and got into bed. As I was lying in the dark, I felt tension in the center of my stomach, and I was flooded by thoughts racing through my mind. Within seconds, I was under a slight weight of sadness. My stomach was in knots. *What the hell is my problem?* (Yes, this is how I speak to myself.) And then it hit me.

I was sick with thoughts of inadequacy.

When I was a child, I had dreams of being a great success. I wanted to be recognized for making a contribution to society. And based on my brilliant accomplishments, I would be afforded the opportunity to travel the world and spoil all those I love with the riches they deserve. But after watching Beyoncé's documentary and seeing everything she has achieved in her young life, not to mention the path she has blazed for the future of her family, I felt like a loser.

Not a loser who seeks to bring down winners because of jealousy— yuck, I hate those losers! I felt like a loser who knows they aren't really a loser, but they're so disheartened that they haven't accomplished as much as they set out to achieve that the only word their ego shouts is "LOSER"!

Please note that I clearly understand that I am *NO* Beyoncé. But I *am* the kind of person who wants to be the best, give the best, and receive the best. And seeing a glimpse into Beyoncé's life was a reminder that I am not where I want to be—and I am no longer at the age where I can say, "When I grow up . . ."

And that is when I called my girlfriend, Shelonda.

You should meet her. She's a dynamo. I compare her to Olivia Pope. She's the type of woman who works hard to provide the best for all those around her. She is a gifted listener, and if she can't fix your problem, she knows someone who can. We were on the phone, and before I knew it, I was pouring my heart out. And, in true Olivia Pope fashion, she was more than ready to fix me.

She shared that her daughter had been begging her for permission to invite a particular classmate over to the house. She was reluctant to give in because you never know how these kids are going to act, and she wasn't too excited about having random children in her home. But she eventually caved! When the little girl arrived, she changed the energy in the room. She was so kind—the most genuine, pleasant, and gracious presence. The type of girl you would want your nine-year-old daughter to be around.

At the end of the evening, my girlfriend loaded everyone in the car to drop off the young lady. After following the GPS, they turned the corner into one of the city's most historically oppressed neighborhoods—full of boarded-up homes and police cameras. They walked to the door, and the little girl's mother greeted them as they entered the small, narrow row home that held the family of six children. The house was in need of drastic repairs, but it was hard to see past the love the family showed for each other.

The point my girlfriend made was there is nothing wrong with wanting more, but don't get so far ahead of yourself that you don't appreciate what you have.

This week I've engaged in a lot of soul-searching conversations with my husband, family, and friends, and they have all echoed the same sentiments. Striving for the best is wonderful—it's what makes

> The moment you start comparing yourself, you lose yourself.

us the driven people we are. We don't settle! But you have to remind yourself that what God has for us is by unique design.

FAR FROM CUTE

With a baby and a three-level home, the amount of "unwanted" exercise that this new mother got was ridiculous. At any given moment, I would have S. Dot in the basement, in the kitchen, in his nursery, back to the basement, now in the living room, and of course when I needed anything of value (i.e., the bib, my Medela lanolin ointment, baby wipes, that miraculous blue "soothie" pacifier, a bottle of water, my cell phone, his favorite tweety rattle, etc.), it was *always* in the room where I wasn't!

To overcome this annoyance, my home uniform became anything loose-fitting with deep pockets. When guests came to visit, they would most often find me in my navy-blue Adidas sweatpants and any shirt that I could quickly slip my arm through and pull out my breast to feed S. Dot. (I know! Graphic, but true.)

Now, would I consider this outfit sexy? Hell no! But was it functional? Most definitely.

Heaven knows, like most women, I would have loved to keep it "Beyoncé chic" every day. But having a fashion sense wasn't much of a priority after being peed on, thrown up on, and having to deal with every other bodily function my son is far too willing to share. And we haven't even discussed the amount of time I spend crawling around on the floor with S. Dot like we are in boot camp.

If it's a choice between cute or comfortable, I'm choosing comfortable EVERY TIME!

GROSS AND GREEDY

My son will pass gas and keep going about his business. I go to change his diaper, and before I have an opportunity to wipe him clean, he's already pulling at his unmentionables waiting to hear me say, "Eww, S. Dot! Stop touching it!" And now he has figured out that snot forms when he cries, so he will spend ten minutes blowing it out of his nose and feeling it ooze onto his lips. *Disgusting!*

I was talking to my girlfriend about it this morning, and she had me cracking up. "Oh guuurl, that's nothing! You just wait until he's older. Then you'll see how gross little boys can really be . . . and not to mention, greedy!"

As quick as the insult flew from her lips, her thirteen-year-old son came barreling down the steps. "Mom, are you going to call me the egg-and-cheese monster again?" Backstory: my girlfriend's son Jonathan is notorious for eating *everything* in sight, leaving only scraps for his sister and mother. One day he was complaining about being hungry, so his mother told him to make some eggs. After he saw that there were four in the carton, he graciously decided to scramble three eggs (with cheese) and leave one for rest of his family.

I'm not ready!

Then, it hit me. I may not want to deal with this, but I think I'll be okay. I grew up with a disgusting and greedy little brother. He's four years younger than me. He prepared me for this life. I remember being fourteen years old. As soon as I would come home from school, my brother would be standing at the door locked and loaded with a barrage of questions: "Was the bus crowded? Did you stop at the store? Do you have any candy? You wore that to school? What's wrong with your hair? Mommy said you have to help me with my homework. When are you going to warm up dinner?" He would chase me to my room with questions until he had me cornered. And that is when I would smell it: a funk that reminds you of the deepest depths of a boy's football locker—the dreaded stench of *sweaty underarms*. I would scream.

Me: BOY, DID YOU PUT ON DEODORANT TODAY?!?

Him: Nope! <spinning with his arms spread out to his sides—the odor filling my room>

Me: OH MY GOD! YOU STINK! <pushing him out the door>

Him: <still spinning> It's my secret weapon!

When it comes down to it, at some point in their lives, most boys are gross. They wipe their nose with their hand. They burp out loud. They find joy in smelling their farts. They hate taking a bath. Deodorant is their archenemy. They find brushing their teeth to be a nuisance. And, on top of that, they eat all of your food.

Am I ready? Yes, because their gross-ness just adds to the list of embarrassing stories we can tell when they're older. And with a little luck (and Speed Stick), they turn out to be clean, respectful, and giving *men*—like my little brother!

Slugs and snails and puppy-dogs' tails—that's what little boys are made of.

WHAT THE DAUGHTER DOES, THE MOTHER DID

Everyone keeps asking me, "When are you having another baby?"

Don't get me wrong, I am not opposed to having another child, but if it were to happen, I'd want another son. I love little boys. My husband has begged me to stop saying that out loud because it sounds creepy, like Chris Hansen may bust into our living room with cameras rolling.

What I am trying to say is that I've always felt I would be a better mother to a boy. Sometimes I think it is because of my close relationship with my younger brother, but most of the time it is because I remember how I was as a child. Have you ever heard the saying, "What the daughter does, the mother did"? Well, that scares the hell out of me. Ask my parents, and they will gladly give you a first-person account of the ridiculous things I did as a child, and the highlight reel gets worse after I hit sixteen. But even as my loving parents are rolling on the floor laughing at my foolishness, I think to myself, *If you only knew the stuff I did and never got caught.* To this day, I still won't say my crimes out loud because I am not sure of the statute of limitations. Olivia Pope couldn't save me from my parents, and I'm grown!

One of my girlfriends is praying hard that my next child is a girl. She believes my daughter would be a better version of myself, a force to be reckoned with. I appreciate the compliment, but I don't have the patience to raise "a force to be reckoned with." That doesn't sound appealing at all.

Don't get me wrong: girls rock! But I'm not jumping at the chance to be responsible for one of them. I'm not good at doing hair, so unless my daughter likes the Sinéad O'Connor look, she's screwed. Little girls are usually into boys before boys even know they exist. Most of these little girls have more breasts, hips, and butt than they know what to do with—and there are plenty of perverts willing to lend a helping hand. And on top of all of this, I'm still haunted by the fact that my mother and I butted heads horribly throughout high school. I don't want to go through that again. To think I will spend hours in labor to push out a little girl who in sixteen years I will want to push off a cliff—no, thank you!

I know I have no control over the sex of my next child. Ultimately, I will be thankful for whoever the Lord blesses me with, but if, on the off chance, Jesus is taking personal requests, I pray there is a little baby penis in my future. Calm down, Chris Hansen. You know what I mean.

One of me is enough!

DON'T MAKE MOMMY ANGRY

I used to think that my mother was a bit psychotic when it came to defending her children. There were times when we were afraid to tell her that someone did something to us because we knew when our mother got started there was no stopping her—she was the female Hulk. But now that I'm a mother, I have a greater respect for my mother's love. To this day, I remember when I realized just how much she loved me.

It was the summer before I entered high school. I was riding my bike with my best friend, while my little brother and his buddies played with their trucks and raced up and down the street. Here is something you need to know: my brother is four years younger than I am. Though he was short for his age, his size had very little effect on how much he ran his mouth. For a nine-year-old, he was a bit of an asshole, but I loved him. He was my annoying shadow, and we both understood that through thick or thin we were each other's responsibility. My mother would accept nothing less than the utmost loyalty between us.

On this particular evening, we were all enjoying our last days of summer, when we had the pleasure of crossing paths with Latonya. Ugh! Tonya. She was two years older than I was, and she just knew she was cute. You know the girls that proudly broadcast that they lost their virginity at the age of five? She couldn't stand me, but if there was anyone she hated more, it was my sharp-tongued brother. Suspiciously, she was walking toward us with a group of older girls. I watched them closely to make sure no one touched my brother. Of course, this bothered Tonya, so she told her friends she was going to whoop my ass. She demanded that I stand there while she went across the street to the store. Um, who in their right mind is going to wait patiently for someone to whoop their ass?

I went back around the corner closer to my house. My father was studying in the kitchen; he never went too far when we were outside. I knew I should have told him what happened, but then he would have made me come in the house. Twenty minutes later, here comes Tonya. Immediately, I felt that fight-or-flight sensation. I always had a good sense of situations, and I could tell I wouldn't be able to talk my way out of this one. She swung on me, and the next thing you know, we were fighting on the concrete. Out the corner of my eye, I saw a four-foot black blur running down the street screaming, "DAAAAAAADDDDDDDY!!!!!"

Though I come from a family of fighters, I hate it. There is something so barbaric about physical altercations, so I try my best to avoid them. But when you're backed into a corner, you have to come out swinging—and that is what I did. After what seemed like hours, I felt someone grab me by my waist, and I kicked and swung with everything in me. Then I was hoisted in the air. My father had me in a bear hug. I was so hyped off adrenaline and raw emotions, the sight of him brought me to tears.

Later that night, I sat in the tub; I was on pins and needles waiting for my mother to get home from work. I think my father and I shared the same fear of my mother finding out, but there was no way to avoid it.

It felt like only seconds before my mother came barreling into the bathroom, checking me for cuts and bruises. She looked manic, crazed in the eyes. She told me to get my clothes on, and before I knew it, she had called the police. Here stood this six-foot, three-inch white police officer in our small kitchen. He looked just as confused as I did.

Officer: Ma'am, I don't think that you can file charges for this altercation.

Mommy: I want this incident noted in your records in case we are ever forced to take extreme measures.

Me and Daddy: <extreme measures?!?>

Officer: Hmm, I don't think it will come to that, ma'am.

But I will let the other parent know that this incident is being noted.

Mommy: I'm going with you.

It's ten p.m. on a Friday night in the middle of the summer. Me, my brother, my father, and my mother are riding in a police car to Tonya's house. We all get out of the car, and the officer knocks on her door. Tonya's mother appears, confused and annoyed. The officer goes on to explain that there will be a public record of the incident that took place. She was appalled.

Her: PUBLIC RECORD?! FOR WHAT?! IT WAS JUST A FIGHT!

Mommy: It was "just a fight" with *my* daughter! And I want it on record in case your daughter makes the mistake of putting her hands on my child again.

Her: I don't know how they do things in the county, but in the city, kids fight all the time!

This was obviously supposed to be an insult. Just because my family carried themselves like we had sense, people in the neighborhood assumed we were from some far distant land—like the county.

Taking two steps toward the open screen door, my mother was a hair's distance from Tonya's mother's face. Gilmore Street fell silent. With a hiss, she whispered, "Read my lips, I'm willing to go to jail for mine. Are you?"

With that, the officer and my father grabbed my mother, leaving Tonya's mother stunned on her front step. My father told the officer we could walk home. The people in the neighborhood stared at us the whole way down. I wanted to crawl under a rock, but at the same time, I felt my mother's primal love and protection of her children. And one day, I hope to leave my son with that same level of embarrassment.

Nothing matches a mother's love—nothing!

DEPRESSION

My Dirty Little Secret

My emotions have always been intense, even when I was a child. I never gave it much thought. I assumed my feelings of depression were normal. With very little effort, I would find myself feeling dark and lonely. But because my parents often spoke of their expectation that I would become a successful, self-sufficient, and strong woman, I buried my sadness to not show weakness. When people were around, I'd tell myself, *It's showtime!* and I would strive to be the most engaging and jovial person in the room. But when the crowd broke, so did I.

When I was about ten years old, my mother shared a poem with me entitled, "We Wear the Mask" by Paul Laurence Dunbar:

> We wear the mask that grins and lies,
> It hides our cheeks and shades our eyes,—
> This debt we pay to human guile;
> With torn and bleeding hearts we smile,
> And mouth with myriad subtleties.
>
> Why should the world be over-wise,
> In counting all our tears and sighs?
> Nay, let them only see us, while
> We wear the mask.

His words were just as deep to me then as they are now. Sometimes, we swallow our emotions and put on a strong face, especially African Americans. I was talking to my husband yesterday, and I told him that it is my opinion that when we think of the things our grandparents and great-grandparents went through, we feel guilty to complain of depression and sadness. It just pales in comparison. My husband, being the comedian that he is, turned to me as if he just realized I was standing there and said, "I think all races acknowledge depression, it's just that Black people didn't start getting health insurance until the early 1970s, so they had some other things to take care of before seeing a shrink." He's so profound. (Please note my sarcasm.)

Whether it was due to limited health insurance or a history of oppression, seeing a doctor because you feel sad was not the answer in my family. We pray, we bury our feelings, and we put on the mask. No need for a doctor. Psychiatrists are for crazy people!

Child, you feel low?! You better read your Bible and drink some water.

Growing up, Jesus and water were the answers to all my ailments. Please do not take me as blasphemous. I believe in God, but sometimes people need a prescription before Psalms.

Where my mother preached faith, Daddy Budda (which is what I call my father) would challenge me to seek balance: "Stop going to such extremes. You should never be so happy that you fall, and you should never be so sad that you aren't able to stand up." Well, that was easier said than done. Fast-forward twenty years later, a round of medication, yoga, and numerous counseling sessions, and I'm much better than I used to be. Being aware of my depression, and not feeling guilty because of it, helped me a great deal. And if I hadn't taken the time to focus on my mental health before becoming a parent, I would have been completely taken by surprise during the first three months of S. Dot's life.

Varying forms of postpartum depression affect nearly 80 percent of first-time mothers, and if you have a history of depression, the symptoms can lead to emotional upheaval. But being aware and prepared can help more than you realize. Yes, when we brought S. Dot home, I was a mess, crying, moping, weeping, sad, and tired. But not once did I consider myself weak or feel ashamed. I called doctors. I confided in my friends. I cried in my aunt's arms, and afterward I looked at my son, and I had faith that I would get through it.

　　See, I'd been here before, and I know
the way out.

Don't wear the
mask so long that
you forget what's
underneath.

EIGHT REASONS I HAVEN'T CALLED BACK

A friend of mine called me on Monday and left me a vague voicemail message, and I did not return her call until Wednesday. When I did, she proceeded to make me feel guilty for not responding as quickly as she expected. She used those sarcastic phrases I have become all too familiar with, like, "Well, I know how important you are" and "Thank you for finding the time to fit me in."

Since I became a parent, there have been a few times the awful thoughts below have run through my mind. Do I always feel this way? Absolutely not! Will some of my family and friends be offended? Most definitely yes! But the ones that understand me know that if they really need me, I'm there, and as for the other 10 percent: "Feel free to leave a message, and I will return your call at my earliest convenience. BEEP!"

Here are eight reasons I haven't called you back:

I'm sorry I haven't called you.

I know you texted me, I responded, then you called me, and I didn't answer. But talking to you on the phone defeats the purpose of texting you in the first place. Don't force my hand.

I'm sorry I haven't called you.

I know you left me a message. I just finished washing my three boys and laid them down for bed. I have a thumping headache from a grueling day at work. My PMS is starting, and I still need to eat, figure out what I'm going to wear tomorrow, take a shower, and fold clothes. This is the first moment I've sat down today. If it's not an emergency, I'm sorry, returning your call is not my first priority.

I'm sorry I haven't called you.

Damn you, social media. I know you saw me "Like"" someone's picture or send a tweet, but please don't take my three smiley faces as a sign that I'm ready to engage in a phone conversation. As a matter of fact, emoticons are the perfect example of a person who is unwilling to use their words.

I'm sorry I haven't called you.

Well, actually I did. I called you as soon as I got in my car to drive home. This is the quietest twenty-five minutes of my day, and I called you——but you didn't answer. Yes, you called me back, but it was twenty-six minutes later. Twenty-six minutes later, I'm already entering the house, balancing my heavy work bag and my purse and carrying four bags of groceries. Twenty-six minutes later, my ears are filled with the screams of a four-year-old shouting at his two-year-old twin brothers to stop touching him, stop taking his toys, and stop touching him (again). Twenty-six minutes later, my hands are already elbow deep in Dawn's dish suds, washing whatever remnants of food off plates that one of these children decided they didn't want to eat. Twenty-six minutes later, my wonderful husband is sharing the painstaking details of his day as my mind fluctuates between the horrible day I just had and the hellish day I have to prepare for tomorrow.

I'm sorry I haven't called you.
I know I sound selfish. I'm making this all about me, when it's you who needs to talk. I feel awful, but the fact of the matter is, I don't have the energy to listen.

I'm sorry I haven't called you.
You said to call you when it was a good time, and to be honest, I haven't found one of those yet.

I'm sorry I haven't called you.
I truly am, because I think about calling you every day. It's to the point that the thought of calling you has become a chore that weighs on my mind because of the guilt I feel from not having done it yet.

I'm sorry I haven't called you.
But I get so few moments of quiet that when I do the only thing I want to do is . . . sleep.

When did selfish become such a bad word? Sometimes you need time for yourself.

I HAVE TO PEE

Have you ever been so tired that you don't feel like going to the bathroom? I mean you are exhausted by the sheer thought of getting up, walking to the bathroom, unzipping your pants, and sitting down?

Have you ever lain in bed and thought so hard about how much you don't feel like going to the bathroom that you actually fall back to sleep?

Have you ever wanted a drink of water before bed, but you would rather go to sleep thirsty than have to wake up in the middle of the night to go to the bathroom?

Have you ever looked at your baby and envied his diapers?

Does a catheter sound appealing to you?

Have you ever held your pee in so long that your bladder goes numb? (Very dangerous.)

If you answered "yes" to any of these questions, please know that you are not alone. Millions of Americans suffer from this medical condition, It's called "Too Tired to Pee"!

For fourteen years, I've made the same request of my husband: "Baby, can you go to the bathroom for me?" just praying that one day it would really be possible.

Sometimes you just don't feel like going.

IF I HAD A CLONE . . .

If I had a clone, how easy it would be.

The things I would accomplish would be no small feat.

The first clone would be dedicated to my son.

She would never tire of reading stories and would always be ready to run.

Still, my list is too long, how will I achieve it?

At least three more clones are surely needed!

One for my job,

Dedicated and true,

She would handle all the crap I hate to do.

The second would be the Cinderella of the crew,

Washing and cleaning and cooking, too.

The third would focus on my personal upkeep.

Push-ups don't do themselves, nor do my hair or my feet.

My brows would stay threaded as well as my top lip.

Basically, this clone keeps me neat and fit.

Yet, my phone is still ringing,

The text messages won't stop,

My family and friends seem to need me a lot.

I need a clone to keep up with the daily drama,

Give a shoulder to cry on,

Loan a few dollars.

So now I'm at five, but something seems odd.

I think I need a few more to balance me off.

Yes, my husband needs tending,

That's two clones at least.

A lady by his side,
But a freak in sheets.
He'll be thankful, I'm sure,
How sweet I can be.
Who said that the clones would only service me?
Now the day is ending,
The to-do list is complete,
And the only thing left for *me* to do is *sleep*.

WHY AM I DOING MATH?

People, we need to quit it with the "baby months." After your child hits the age of one, it is my opinion that we should only account for the individual months when absolutely necessary. Some people take it too far! Why do I have to do math in order to figure out how old your kid is?

> **Me:** Oh, he's so cute. How old is he?
>
> **Her:** He's twenty-two months in one week.
>
> **Me:** Huh?!?

Honestly, just say he's almost two years old so I can go on about life. Now, I'm standing in front of a mother I barely know doing long division. Call me rude, but I don't care enough about your child to do arithmetic.

Then, you have the parents that try to use the "months" system as an advantage. My husband and I were in the park, and a little girl roughly the same size as our son S. Dot walked past, playing with her toy. Of course, now my one-year-old is focused on what she is holding in her hands. He walks over, and the little girl's mother turns to her daughter and says, "Honey, are you going to share your toy with the little boy?" Her daughter responds very eloquently, "No!"

I was shocked, not because she didn't want to share (what child really wants to share?) but by how clearly she spoke and understood the question. I asked her parents, "Wow! How old is your daughter?" The father responded, "She's one year old." My heart sank. My son is one, too, and the only word he uses with full understanding is "Huh?"

I felt dizzy. Seconds felt like hours as I began second-guessing my parenting skills. *Why isn't my son speaking as well as this one-year-old girl?* Next thing you know, the mother leans over the father and says, "Well, she's actually twenty months." ARE YOU FREAKING KIDDING ME RIGHT NOW?! After hearing this, I could have honestly slapped the child's father. There is a big-ass difference between a one-year-old and a damn near two-year-old child (excuse my French, but I was HOT!). The father was trying to pull the old okie-doke, having me believe his child is some kind of prodigy while mine is an ogre who uses random grunts, babbles, and screams to communicate.

All I'm saying is let's use months within reason. After your child reaches the age of one, feel free to round up or note halves—but anything further should result in a calculator across the head. Seriously, have you ever heard a person say, "Woo-hoo! It's my 384-month birthday!" No. You know why? Because that person would be considered a douche. Parents: don't be douches!

> Don't try to pull the old okie-doke on me and my baby!

PUT MY BABY AT THE TOP OF THE LIST

I was having lunch with my girlfriend Gozi and we were discussing the pressure of being mothers. We would love to stay home with our children, but financially that is not feasible. Then, the conversation shifted to how expensive these little people are. And did you know that on top of washing and feeding them, you are expected to have them educated? Jeesh! When does it end with these kids?!?

I am going on record, right now, as the creator of a new movie premise. The film will be entitled *The List*, and it will be based on new parents who have to scramble to get their child into the best daycare, best nursery school, and best elementary school to ensure they are in the best position to go to the best college, which will allow them to live the best life ever! *<Sigh>*

OH MY GOD! These "lists" are unbelievable. It's real in these parenting streets. And to think, my husband and I are just getting started!

Do you know how many $50 deposits we will never see again because we had to submit an application fee just to get on the list?

At seven months, we took S. Dot to a walk-though at a preschool, and the instructor informed us that we were late in the "exploring process." REALLY?!? I just gave birth to this child yesterday. How are we late? She went on to explain that most parents start researching schools and programs during pregnancy. WTF?!? I swear I was going to put hands on her, but after a deep breath, I realized it was unlikely that physical assault would help S. make the list.

I have always considered myself to be on top of things, but the search for daycare programs and schools is a daunting task for protective parents.

And guess what, sometimes making "The List" is the least of your worries. Do you know how much some of these programs cost? We are talking about mortgage payments, people! I read a CNN report that stated the average child born today will cost a parent roughly $235,000 by the time the child is seventeen years old, and based on some of the schools I'm seeing, I think $235K was a low estimate.

S. Dot is a year and a half, and I don't think I would be as mildly sane as I am if it weren't for parents who are willing to share information and give inside tips. Everyone wants to be on the right list, but I am reminding myself to breathe and remember that as long as S. Dot is at the top of our list, my baby is going to be all right!

These lists will not be the death of me!

COMPLAIN AT YOUR OWN RISK

I have a friend, Moneé. No matter how upset, frustrated, or annoyed I become with my husband, her advice is always the same: "Work it out because there ain't nothing out here!"

Today, I was complaining to her about my husband, who had just left town for business. I love him dearly, but last night I was looking forward to putting S. Dot to bed and having the entire house to myself. I had just poured a glass of wine, I looked horrible in the most comfortable way, and I was feeling good. But just as soon as I turned on the baby monitor and settled in for a little "me time," the phone rang. It was my husband. He was calling to check in, though we had just finished talking face-to-face on our iPhones forty-five minutes ago.

Every minute we spoke felt like hours. All I could think about was the list of things I had been dreaming of doing over the next two hours. Two hours, people! One hundred and twenty minutes. You don't realize how fast they go when you're actually enjoying yourself. Two whole hours!

As a working mother, that's all I get. I am up and moving from the moment I open my eyes at five a.m. Those two hours are precious. And my husband knows how much I value that time. So, for him to call during my sacred two hours to chitchat because he's bored is frustrating.

Don't look at me like that. You are the one who chose to read my diary. I know you're probably thinking exactly what she was thinking: "Um, I'm sorry. Are you complaining because your man called to check on you?!"

Did I mention that my friend is single without children?

<continue music>

Moneé has an imaginary scorecard she uses when I complain about motherhood or marriage, and let's just say my husband and son are having a hell of a season!

I have found that I have to be careful complaining to some of my friends, because life's challenges are a matter of perspective. Something that's an issue for you wouldn't amount to a hill of beans to someone else. Short of my husband laying hands on me, I will never get sympathy from Moneé (nor should I), because in her eyes I have someone who loves and supports me, and to focus on anything else is a complete waste of time.

Don't call Moneé!

WHERE AM I?

Here's some honesty for you. We're two weeks away from selling our home—which has been an ordeal in and of itself. And guess what? We still haven't found a new house. So, now we're faced with the dilemma of being all packed up with nowhere to go.

This is in addition to dealing with the worst first trimester a woman could ask for. I'm talking all-day nausea, migraines, soreness, constipation, exhaustion, extreme swelling, congestion, heartburn—oh, and did I mention *all-day nausea*?!?

There are days I'm literally numb with pain. And it's not as if I can just call out from work. Let me paint a picture for you. After lying on the floor of my bathroom from four a.m. to six a.m., hugging the toilet like I'm reuniting with a close friend, I arrive in the office at 7:30 a.m. to a group of coworkers who revel in talking loudly about absolutely nothing!

Seriously, aside from my breasts getting bigger (which are the only thing on my body worth looking at), this pregnancy is for the birds!

And guess whose son decided that now was a good time to test-drive the terrible twos?

S. Dot has become the fussiest man-child we've ever come in contact with. We have actually changed his name to the Dictator because all he does is aggressively demand things and walk around exerting his tyranny. He can't speak English, though judging by his rants he clearly doesn't know that. I swear my son sounds like a mix between Kim Jong-il and Hitler. It's very unsettling.

I digress. What I'm trying to say is that I'm in a state of flux right now (along with acid reflux). I can't write as much as I would like, but once things calm down and we unpack my computer, I have a lot to share.

I want to do it all, but admitting that I can't is a true sign of maturity.

WHEN THE JUGGLER FALLS

I'm a juggler. I pride myself on being able to handle multiple tasks and not drop one. The key is staying as emotionally stable as possible. As long as I don't freak out, I can juggle all day and not break a sweat. But a few weeks ago, everything crashed around me.

I didn't feel well for most of February. Last year, I had my thyroid removed, so I am often tired, but I take B-12 supplements to help maintain my energy. We are currently in the middle of selling our home and trying to purchase a new one, which means numerous showings with very little notice, and this is all in addition to having an energetic eighteen-month-old son and a full-time job. I've been physically drained for weeks.

One weekend my husband decided that we needed a date night to try to lift my spirits and reconnect. As we sat in the restaurant, the room started spinning. I never get dizzy, but here I was holding onto the table with my eyes closed. I turned to my husband and immediately started crying. The thought hit me like a ton of bricks; exhaustion, emotional, dizzy: *I'm f@king pregnant!*

My husband and I stopped at the grocery store. I could not believe I was actually walking down an aisle to purchase a test that would determine if I was going to bring *another* child into this world. Everything around me seemed brighter, which I believe is the first sign of a stroke. Oddly, my husband was walking five steps behind me, as if the distance from my womb buffered the shock.

Later that night, after placing S. Dot in bed, I went into the

bathroom and had the most important pee of my life, and within seconds—just like the box said—our fate was determined.

My husband walked in, and with a smirk, he uttered, "That is the strongest purple line I've ever seen. It's so purple it's black!" He was right. It was as if the test was screaming, "NO NEED FOR A SECOND OPINION, DARLING! YOUR ASS IS SUPER PREGNANT!"

Sweet Black baby Jesus!

WOMEN WITHOUT CHILDREN ARE SELFISH

[Standing in line at Bank of America with S. Dot. An older lady stands behind us.]

> **Her:** Your son is so handsome!
>
> **Me:** Aww, thank you very much. I appreciate that.
>
> **Her:** You just don't see enough women like you having children.
>
> **Me:** <Hmm, I'm not sure I like where this is going.>
>
> **Her:** Women get educated and decide they don't want to have babies. It's just selfish!
>
> **Me:** <Cautiously> I can't say that I agree. It's not selfish; it's their choice.
>
> **Teller:** I can help the next person in line.
>
> **Me:** <Thank God!>

I always told myself I wasn't going to have children. My plan was to move to New York, purchase a loft apartment, become a power player in marketing, make a decent living, get a Chinese Shar-Pei, and date when I was bored. And on any given day, that still sounds like a great plan.

But that wasn't my path, and I have absolutely *no* regrets. I love my little family. But if another woman told me that having a family was not what she wanted for her life, I would not dare call her selfish. Heck, I only have one child, and not a moment goes by that I am not racking my brain stressed about how we are going to protect him from the craziness in this world, how to find the money to pay for daycare, nursery school, private school, college, how to ensure he is smart enough not to be trapped by some of these "hot in da tail" girls, and heaven forbid if my husband and I can no longer see eye to eye— raising a child alone can be a struggle.

So, if a woman decides that bringing a child into this world is not something that she is comfortable with, she should be supported, not scolded.

It is my opinion that "selfish" is consciously having a child and knowing that you are not prepared to handle the responsibility. Selfish is having a baby because you think it's fun or because your friends have one. Selfish is becoming pregnant in order to keep a person who does not want you. I can give you a list of a million things that are selfish, but a woman who decides not to have a child because she does not feel she is ready is not one of them.

Do you, BooBoo!

SO YOU HAD A BAD DAY?

Have you ever had dark thoughts? I mean the type of thoughts that make it hard for you to look in the mirror or consider yourself a good person. Those are the kind of thoughts I've been battling for months. I've been so consumed with sadness that it has been easier to talk about everything else but the one thing that is truly bothering me.

Why?

Because there is nothing worse than when a person catches you when you've hit your bottom. It's the equivalent of crying at work. (I HATE CRYING AT WORK!)

But I've realized that I'm being a hypocrite. This is my diary. Why waste time lying to myself? I tell stories because I want to create a world where good people could have bad days and not feel judged.

I'm not in a good place right now.

You may decide that this is a book you would rather not finish. If so, I respectfully understand.

You can't have a testimony without a test.

COME AGAIN?!

(Part One of "Expecting a Baby")

On March 18, my husband and I were beyond excited to attend our first ultrasound appointment. The thought that we were having another child was a little overwhelming but amazing at the same time. Now that he was closer to two years old, we wanted S. Dot to have a partner in crime. This crawling on the floor and being his main form of entertainment was becoming a bit much. Plus, I often tell people that I am not sure how I could have survived childhood without my little brother. After everything we had been through and witnessed while growing up, it is great to have someone who you can talk trash to about your parents. And knowing how crazy I am as a mother, S. Dot is going to need to vent. Having a second child would save him money on therapy later.

The doctor estimated that we were at seven weeks, five days. And now it was time for the big reveal. I laid back, and she inserted the ultrasound wand.

(**Side note:** We have all had sex before, right? We know the positions that are required, but everything changes when a woman has to go to the OBGYN. Okay, maybe it's me, but it feels foreign, damn near indecent, to be asked to strip from your waist down, cover yourself in an oversized paper towel, and have your legs spread in a brightly lit sterile room. There is *nothing* sexy about the doctor's office—nothing! When my husband is with me, I always tell him to close his eyes.)

> **Him:** I've seen you before. How do you think we got into this position?!
>
> **Me:** \<pause\> Well, it was under better lighting and wine was involved.

I digress. I lay back, and the doctor began the exam. For a second, I couldn't tell what was up or down on the screen. It looked like I was watching a sunny side-up egg come in and out of focus on the monitor. The doctor paused and asked if we saw what she did. We looked closely, but nothing was clear. She said that what we were seeing were two heartbeats: "You're having twins!" Instantly, the room went pitch-black as my eyes closed, feebly attempting to hold back the instant flood of hot tears. The sound of my heartbeat filled my ears. A sharp pain seared across my temples. I started hyperventilating. I felt my stomach lurch into a ball of knots. My world felt like it was crashing around me. In that second, the way I imagined my life unfolding, the plans I had made, all shattered like exploding picture frames. My husband saw my horror and tried to embrace me, but the compression of the news made my body go rigid. The doctor scrambled to leave the room to give us a moment alone, but looking back, I wonder if a part of her was frightened by my reaction.

I let out a silent scream. I was inconsolable. After taking the pregnancy test a few weeks prior to our doctor's visit, I had been feeling very sick and extremely tired. I chalked it up to the normal side effects of the first trimester—I had experienced extreme nausea and exhaustion for the first four months of my pregnancy with S. Dot—but still something in my spirit told me that this was different. Though I was only a few weeks pregnant, I felt as if I had been pregnant for months. I vomited constantly. I couldn't go up a flight a of steps without feeling the need to sleep for hours.

My head throbbed and my body hurt. The pain was so awful there were times I thought about sticking a safety pin in my hand to distract my mind. Sound crazy? Maybe, but I saw it in a movie. What can I say, I was desperate. Here's how I would compare describe it: Have you ever read *Twilight*? If you haven't, spoiler alert! During Bella's pregnancy in *Breaking Dawn*, everything accelerated. It took only hours for the fetus to grow, not months, and it was too much for Bella's human body to bear. The baby was literally tearing her apart from the inside out. Now, I'm not saying I thought I was giving life to a vampire, but it sure as hell felt like it. I was being drained and experiencing the worst pregnancy in a rapid-fire cocktail of symptoms.

As the news of the twins hit me, it all started to make sense. And at the same time, it didn't. What was happening to me? I didn't want twins. I couldn't handle twins. It felt as if my uterus was being invaded. I was praying that the Lord would bless me with another beautiful baby boy, and now I had been cursed with the crushing blow of bringing two children into the world. Yes, I said cursed. At the time, I did not feel that I was receiving a blessing. How could I raise three children? I wanted to give my second child everything I gave my first. I was going to give birth naturally, breastfeed for at least three months, and pump for a year. After having S. Dot, I felt that I was better prepared, and I was looking forward to relishing every moment of my second pregnancy, showing off my baby bump, and enjoying it. Now I felt that it was all being stripped from me. Not to mention that my husband and I were in the middle of selling our home and looking for a house for our soon-to-be family of four. Now I'm being told there would be five of us. As I cried in my husband's arms, I felt a shift in my being. I wasn't the same person who had walked through the doctor's door an hour ago. And the weeks that followed showed me the true depths of my dark mind.

WTF

THE DARK SIDE

(Part Two of "Expecting Twins")

Despite the encouraging support of my husband, family, and close friends, I could not accept how much my life was going to change with the news of expecting twins.

Not only was I as sick as a dying dog, but I was also sick of hearing, "This is a blessing." Or, "If there is anyone who can do this, it's you!" Oh, and my favorite, "The Lord only gives you as much as you can bear." That one really pissed me off. I don't want to go through life "bearing."

As these words would flow from their mouths, all I could picture was Atlas, from Greek mythology. Just because I have the ability to carry the world on my shoulders doesn't mean I want to. And that was exactly my issue. I didn't *want* to have twins. I didn't *want* the responsibility of nursing and raising two children at the same time. I couldn't wrap my head around the amount of work in store for me and my husband. I questioned whether we were built for this. Hell, after five months of having S. Dot, my husband and I were already toying with the idea of divorce. (Sleep deprivation is a b@#$%!)

This news had me reeling. Every time I looked at my son, I would burst into tears. I felt that I was crowding him out. How would I possibly give S. Dot the attention and love he deserved when I was struggling to get both of my nipples into my twins' mouths, and this is after being up for seventy-two hours straight with nothing to eat but a handful of Special K cereal? And let's not talk about MONEY! How were we going to afford three f@#%ing children?

Our intention was to have a second child, move to a slightly larger home, and live happily ever after. Didn't God get my memo?

All my life I have been criticized for being too much of a planner. Now, people were using the trait they once chastised me about as a great reason for me to be "blessed" with multiples. "Oh, you're going to be great with twins because the key is scheduling." I wanted to say, "Screw you. The key is not losing my damn mind and jumping off a bridge!"

The doubt in my head and the fear in my heart were overpowering. The more depressed I became, the more guilty some people made me feel. I didn't appreciate how casually they were treating my feelings. No one seemed to realize how saddened and dark I had become—except for my husband. He was the most caring, sensitive, and understanding man a woman could ask for. He didn't speak of the pregnancy because he knew it would set me off. He took over most of the responsibilities with S. Dot because I was too physically ill to move. I only did three things: go to work, come home, and get in bed. He hid the ultrasound pictures because he knew the sight of our reality was too much for me to process. He comforted me when I would randomly burst into hysterical tears. And he sat silently the night I came home and asked him, "Would you be able to forgive me if I decided to terminate this pregnancy?"

Personally, all my life, I've believed an abortion was never an option for me. My conscious faith wouldn't allow it. But here I was in my dark and twisty place, contemplating taking the life of two children because I thought I was only built to handle one. It was as difficult for me to say as it was for my husband to hear.

When you look at the dark side, careful you must be . . .
for the dark side looks back.

—Yoda

BOXING WITH GOD

(Conclusion of "Expecting Twins")

Once I had spoken the word *abortion* to my husband, it was as if the effect echoed throughout the house. For weeks, it had been a thought that crawled through my mind, lurking in the shadows of my oversized doubt, fear, and insecurities. I tried to swat it away like a fly and ignore its presence, but it was relentless.

Ironically, though it was difficult to say out loud, I felt a sense of relief in releasing it. It forced me to face it.

Looking into my husband's eyes, I could see his inner struggle. He told me that ultimately this is my body and my decision, but he honestly felt that God would provide.

At this point, my husband and I had been together for fourteen years. Over that time, we'd weathered many storms and come out the other side a little battle weary but stronger nonetheless. It has actually become our mantra, as a couple, that "we handle our business." My husband looked at the news of the twins as another testament of our strength.

For the next week, I went through my days on autopilot. I have an uncanny ability to shut down my emotions while still being able to engage people. I'm not saying it with pride; it just is what it is. I actually got this trait from my mother. When I was very young, she would tell me, "The world doesn't need to know your business. When you enter a room, you tell yourself, 'It's showtime!' leaving those around you none the wiser." And that is what I did. I went to work, led meetings, did presentations, and attended evening events, and then I would come home and go silent. Those closest to me told me to pray, but it is hard to confide in someone that you are mad with. Yes, I was mad at God. I was angry and frustrated. And one night, I exploded. I went off! I cursed and screamed and cried, and after falling to sleep with swollen eyes, I woke up and went to the bathroom. I looked at myself in the mirror and remembered a Def Poet performer, Flow Mentalz, who wrote a poem about boxing with God. It told the story of a physical battle a man had with God, attacking God for all the unfairness in his life and the world. After twelve gruesome rounds, the man had landed many heavy blows upon God, but God didn't seem affected. At the end of the fight, God gave the tired man a mirror, and through swollen eyes the man saw that it was he who was bloody and bruised. He had been fighting himself all along because God was within him.

At that moment, I decided to shake the darkness and treat the news of having twins as a gift versus a curse.

I can't imagine my life without S. Dot, but there was a time I would have cringed at the mere mention of having children. Now look at me. I would give my life without a moment's thought to save and protect my son.

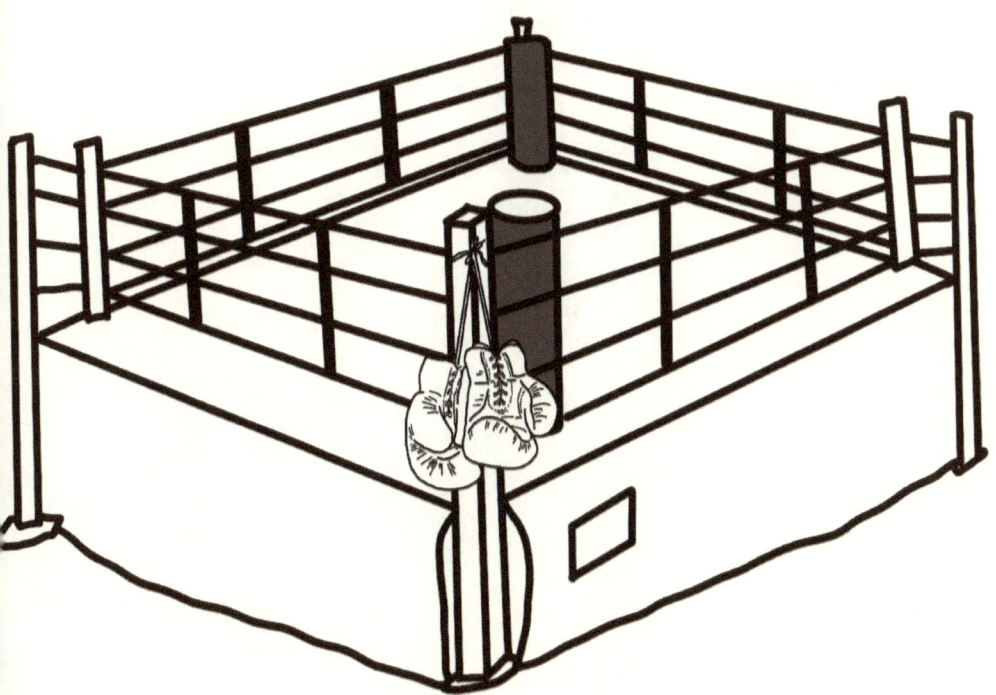

I realized I had to have enough faith to know that God would not leave me now, and that I had the strength within me to handle this.

A week later, I was in the shower, and I heard one of my favorite songs, "To Zion," by the phenomenally gifted Ms. Lauryn Hill. I sung along smiling, holding my protruding belly, crying uncontrollably. In my spirit, I felt God speaking to me, "Gurl, you've got this, because I've got you."

You imbecile, don't you know you're a reflection of God?

I THINK I LOVE MY JOB

I consider myself an exceptional worker. (I have the employee evaluations to prove it.) I show up every day fired up and ready to go. If a coworker makes a request, I follow up immediately; and if my boss asks me to lend an extra hand, I don't shy away. Bottom line: I take my position and my job seriously. After having my son, my mentality is no different. But I do believe expectations should be adjusted when a parent returns to the workplace after having a child.

Now, with three children, I'm not the same worker I was seven years ago. Then, I was younger. I had no attachments and no commitments. It was easier to be all things to all people, because I had no one in my personal life who required my full attention. This meant I could dedicate more to my career.

"So, you decided to wait until the end of the day to ask me to follow up on something that requires more time than I currently have? Not a problem."

"I recognize this is not in my job description, but to prove my value to this organization, I am going to spend my Friday, Saturday, and Sunday at this festival lifting boxes, chatting with complete strangers, and loading my car in 100-degree heat just to demonstrate I'm a team player."

"Oh, instead of YOU going, you want to send ME to represent the company at a boring event from five to nine tonight? Count me in!"

"You asked other departments to complete projects, and they didn't, so instead of reprimanding or firing them, you would like to delegate their work to me, in addition to what I am already responsible for? Sounds fair!"

Don't get me wrong: I understand that I will always face the challenge of having to prove myself—and this is an obstacle I have no doubt I will overcome (because I'm a beast). But as a working mother who values her reputation of being good, capable, and reliable, it is difficult to say no in the workplace. I feel that I will be viewed as a slacker if I say, "I cannot do that because I have no one to watch my son," or "No, this will have to wait until tomorrow because my son goes to bed at seven p.m., and I don't want to miss another night of not being able to tuck him in." Man, sometimes working full-time in the field I love, while being a mother, is a real balancing act.

It is not the responsibility of my employer to care about my personal life, it's mine.

A MOTHER ON THE VERGE OF EXPLODING

Have you ever been hit with so much bulls#$% you think, *I could write a book?*

The challenge is that life comes at you so fast that some parents struggle to find the time to tend to their own sanity. We go on autopilot because life doesn't grant you a time out or a do-over.

I'm serious. Give me ten seconds, and I can name at least ten absolutely amazing mothers who are seconds away from exploding every day. I swear, in their mind it's a constant question of which wire to cut, the red or the green one?

And I can relate. I'm on bed rest due to a high-risk pregnancy with twins, working from home, with a two-year-old son and an overworked husband who is balancing his responsibilities of being a father and being a man with career aspirations.

I have some family and friends who get me; they don't crowd me, but support me. They meet me where I am and never attempt to force me to be someone I'm not. But on the other hand, I am dealing with some people who have their own agenda, and they selfishly find ways to turn situations around to make *everything* about what they want and expect—causing me stress and strain in the wake of their inconsideration.

Frankly speaking, I'm negotiating detonation on a daily basis.

I have so much to say, but so little capacity to tell it.

Tick . . . tick . . . tick . . . tick.

THIRTY-FOUR WEEKS WITH TWINS

They Said I'd Be Lucky to Make It

I was thirty-four weeks pregnant with twin boys. Seven weeks earlier, that would have seemed unlikely.

At twenty-seven weeks, I was rushed to Labor and Delivery because I was two and a half centimeters dilated and experiencing strong contractions, though I didn't feel a thing.

Here I was thinking I was coming in for a routine ultrasound, and BAM! They had me rolling through triage in a wheelchair.

As I've mentioned before, I avoid hospitals at all costs. I acknowledge their benefits, but they make me very uncomfortable. I had a friend who lived and breathed the emergency room. She could have an eyelash in her eye and she would call 911. I'm not kidding! She would do it because she needed the attention—she enjoyed having everyone rushing to the hospital to be by her bedside and cater to her every need. Unless vanity is a medical condition, I say toss her a bottle of Visine and keep it moving.

As for me, if I have a choice of curing myself or bearing the pain, the last place I am going is to a hospital. I swear if my husband wasn't so against me giving birth at home, we'd deliver these boys in our living room.

I digress.

At twenty-seven weeks, I was told I had an "irritable uterus," which is a funny term, if you ask me.

Pelvis: I hate working with that damn Uterus. She's always walking around with her face screwed up—making things difficult for everyone. Hehe!

The doctors stated I was experiencing preterm labor, and if they could not stop it soon, the babies would be born premature. They would be at risk for many complications. I was given doses of indomethacin and nifedipine, along with two steroid shots in my thigh to help the twins' lungs develop. Then they told me I had to stop working and remain in the hospital for two weeks.

Errr! <record scratch> You want me to stop what? And stay where?

I was horrified—literally, in tears. I felt as if everything was spinning out of control. Everyone was telling me to think about what was best for the babies, as if that was not my intention. But no one understood that I needed to work in order to take care of these babies. Don't get me wrong: my husband is Superman, but our Fortress of Solitude is still a two-income household.

I was hit with too much information at one time and expected to process everything immediately.

Nurse: Call your job and tell them you won't be back.
Nurse: Do you have final names?
Nurse: Do you have two car seats with you?
Nurse: Do you have a birth plan?

I wanted to scream, "B@#$%, I'm six months pregnant with a nearly two-year-old son waiting for me at home, and I just started *trying* to get used to the idea of even having three children. What makes you think I have a birth plan? That's the problem: I didn't plan to have this kind of birth!"

I stayed in the hospital overnight, restricted to using a very sexy metal bedpan because I wasn't allowed to walk. In time, with the help of the medications, the contractions seemed to lessen. So, the next morning, I announced I was leaving. Yes! Leaving.

The idea of me staying in the hospital for two weeks to simply be "monitored" was ridiculous. My son was turning two years old in one week, and I was not missing his birthday. Life was still going on around me. And if my twenty-four hours on the Labor and Delivery floor showed me anything, it was that I still had a lot of things to get in order before the arrival of these two boys. Plus, sitting in an uncomfortable hospital bed, in uncomfortable hospital clothes, and eating horrible hospital food just wasn't appealing to me. I would better serve my babies by being in a place that relaxed me, like the comfort of my own home.

The reality is, the longer you stay in a hospital, the more the hospital gets paid from the insurance company. And this mommy refuses to stay anywhere for two weeks just so you can look at me.

I know my body, and I know how to follow directions. Just tell me when to take the medication, and I will call you if I experience any pain. But until then, I'm out!

So, that's my story. I discharged myself from the hospital. Yet, I did compromise. My company graciously offered me the opportunity to work from home, which was a blessing.

At thirty-four weeks, my babies were roughly five pounds each and doing very well. As for me, that was another story.

Listen. Know your body. And use common sense.

I'M TIRED OF BEING PREGNANT

My first pregnancy with S. Dot could be considered a sweet dream compared to the experience I am having with twins.

Sometimes I blame my attitude. Not a day goes by that I don't question, *How the hell am I going to raise three boys? I know, I know . . . this is a blessing. I should be happy, right?* Well, you tell that to my swollen hands, face, feet, ankles, and legs. I look like a drowning victim. Tell that to the very active five-and-a-half-plus-pound boys weighing down on my pelvis with so much pressure it feels as if someone drop-kicked me in the vagina. Tell that to the sciatic nerve pain in my lower back that buckles my knees and makes me curse the gods whenever I walk, sit, roll over, bend down, stand up, and basically do anything that would classify me as an able-bodied human being. Tell that to the pockets of tender varicose veins on my legs, which my two-year-old son lovingly refers to as "MiMi's boo-boos." Tell that to the heartburn. My God, the heartburn: the searing feeling in your upper chest as the acidic, salty taste of spit fills the back of your throat. Tell that to the vomit. My apologies, "regurgitation." Hell, no matter what you call it, it's disgusting. It's unnatural to kneel on the floor with your face in the same area people rest their butts to pee and poop. People assume that because you are eating for three people you have a huge appetite. Seriously?!? I have two baby boys crammed into my belly; there's no space for my stomach. There's no room for a big meal. And when you have constant heartburn, fuhgeddaboudit. As soon as the food goes down, it comes right back up. Yeah, you think I should be happy—tell that to the hemorrhoids. (Need I go on?) Tell that to my racing heart, which (out of nowhere) will randomly pound like a thoroughbred race-horse, leaving me with shortness of breath and dizziness, and seeing spots. All I can say is, "I'm coming to join you, Elizabeth!"

Oh, and let's not forget the emotional toll. Not to say I wasn't a sensitive human being before, but now I can go from zero to sixty in seconds. My irritability threshold gets lower and lower every day. I work so hard to hold back tears that I feel the levees will break at any moment.

And my triggers are simple. Take, for example, my son. I can't be the mommy I used to be for him. Yes, S. Dot may sit for a few minutes to listen to me read him a story, but he is a vibrant and energetic little boy. He wants to be chased around the room and wrestled to the ground. Mommy can't do that! Mommy is too sore and too tired. It kills me to know that these are my last few days of just me and my firstborn child, and I am not able to do everything I want with him.

When I found out I was pregnant with our second child, I was ecstatic. I wanted S. Dot to have a partner, and because I knew what to expect from pregnancy, I was looking forward to enjoying the experience more this time around . . . but learning I was having twins was a shock and an adjustment I still have not quite accepted. Honestly, if I had to do it over again, I am not confident of my answer.

Don't ask me how I'm doing unless you know how to play the violin.

EARLY PARENTHOOD

Perception vs. Reality

Most people would consider me to be a fairly self-sufficient woman. I take pride in going in alone and handling my business. And therein lies the problem. I've allowed my "perception of strength" to fool me into believing that asking for help is a weakness. I heard a quote once that knocked me on my behind: "If you are too proud to admit you are hurting, don't be surprised if no one seems to care."

The week following my twins' birth was the hardest time of my life. See, I'm not a fan of hospitals, which makes me a horrible patient. I had an emergency C-section on Wednesday afternoon, and, against my husband's and family's advice, I checked myself out of the hospital thirty-six hours later. After months of bed rest, hospital stays, and scares, I just wanted to go home. But once there, reality hit that I wasn't in good shape. The pressure in my head was so bad I couldn't move my body without seeing stars and feeling searing pain shoot down my neck and spine. Every step I took, I felt the floor shift under my feet. I couldn't keep anything down, and the more I vomited, the worse my head throbbed and my abdominal stitches stretched. Compounded by the physical pain, I was sleep-deprived, my hormones were depleted, and I felt trapped by two screaming, fragile newborns and a two-year-old toddler who was struggling to process the change. With all sincerity, I didn't think I was going to make it; either the pain or the stress was going to kill me.

Two weeks later, my cousins expressed their disappointment in me for not hosting Thanksgiving dinner. A friend responded to my text that she couldn't visit me because she was in too bad a mood. And then there were friends and family who either didn't call me or called with problems.

My husband came home from work one afternoon to find me exhausted and crying while breastfeeding both twins. I was devastated that so few people seemed to give a damn that I was struggling. No one cared that I needed to sleep, that I needed to eat, or that I could use some friendly company. No one cared because no one knew. Everyone assumed that I was okay because that's how I've always carried it. And whose fault is that? Mine.

We've all experienced this in one way or another. Your friends think you're in a happy relationship when at home you and your partner barely speak. Your family has the notion that you're swimming in money, but they don't understand how hard you work to still live paycheck to paycheck. Colleagues swear you're in a position of power, but they're not aware of the daily microaggressions you battle in your career. The world believes you're so put together, but it doesn't see your missing pieces.

Well, not me. Not anymore. I am learning that people appear to us in the shade we throw upon colors. I can't afford to be blinded.

Speak up!

TAKE THESE BABIES . . . PLEASE!

If you have never threatened to throw your baby out of a window, put them in the dryer, or leave them on a stranger's doorstep, then congratulations, you're a better parent than I am.

Look, I know the only way babies have of communicating their needs is through crying, but after a while, something's got to give.

After you have changed them, fed them, burped them, and rocked them while humming every song in the book, you would think that the natural progression would be for the baby to fall asleep, right? No. Babies defy logic. Believe me, when you have done all that you physically can to soothe your child, there is nothing more mind-numbing than listening to them scream at the top of their lungs at three o'clock in the morning. No, the baby does not have colic or diaper rash. No, they don't have an ear infection or sore gums. The baby is just screaming to scream. Oh, and don't forget to multiply those high-pitched shrills times two. (Lucky me!)

After a few weeks with my twin boys, I was convinced that they were members of a military sleeper cell, sent by the government to torture me—miniature terrorists using sleep deprivation to break my spirit and free will. But luckily, I am blessed with a strong support system consisting of my husband, family, and friends, who bring me food and allow me to take naps and long showers. I have people in my life who are willing to help me, because help is what is needed in raising a child—especially three of them.

I often think about the young teenage girls I see pushing baby strollers, their eyes blurred by their new reality. A person who brings a child into the world unprepared for the responsibility could not fathom the toll parenting takes on your life. In those moments in the dark holding my screaming twins, postpartum depression spinning my hormones into a cyclone of rage, I think of the women who snapped. Their intentions were good, but they simply were not equipped for the challenge. You think to yourself, *That would never be me,* but I've had my moments, those times when I had to walk away from my screaming twins—shut the bedroom door, go into the bathroom, sit on the edge of the tub and hang my head. In those moments, God has given me the clarity of mind to step away and breathe.

Raising a child is not easy. I have a two-year-old son and twin newborn boys. Every day I wake up with all three of my children smiling is a blessing, yet I can't help but think about those parents who were brought to the edge and had no one to pull them back.

> You don't know the length of the fall until you jump.

CAN'T A WOMAN HAVE BOUNDARIES?

I just got off the phone with a friend of mine who has a knack for pointing out flaws I never knew I had. (What can I say? She's a gem.) I was sharing with her my recent argument about people not respecting my need for space and time. Toward the end of my tirade, I said, "I mean, it's not that I'm standoffish; I just have boundaries."

Her: But you are standoffish!

Me: What?! No, I'm not.

Her: What do you think "boundaries" means? <insert sarcasm> "A person who wants to stand with others"?

Me: <silence> <deep breath>

Her: Don't be offended. I respect it.

I was taken aback. I've never looked at myself that way. But now, as I faced being a mother to multiples, I had to take a cold hard look at myself.

Do you know what scares me most about having twins? It's not the delivery. It's not the breastfeeding. It's the people who want to help. The expectation of opening up my doors (and myself) to people.

Crazy, right? Well, to understand my statement, you have to understand me. If I have not been allowed the space and time to firmly understand what I'm dealing with, it is difficult for me to tell you how to help me. And if I don't feel you respect the way I prefer things handled, I'd rather take the time to simply do it myself.

By now, you probably think I'm a real nut. But hear me out.

As I child, growing up in West Baltimore, I learned that there are some people who only give in order to get. They have no concept of personal space or boundaries. They force their way into people's lives. They keep a tally of the favors given and always look for their opportunity to cash in. They will be there in your most vulnerable time but later bring it up with the intention of embarrassing and hurting you. It can be like the mafia; you never want to be indebted.

Believe me, if you're around that kind of energy long enough, you can become jaded and psychotically self-sufficient. Your boundaries become your protection—and a violation is taken as pure disrespect. So, you draw lines in the sand. Here are some of mine:

I don't allow S. Dot to drink from other people's cups. And I don't like it when people offer their cup to him. Boundaries.

My husband and I have established a schedule/rules/order that work for our household, and we don't appreciate our rules being challenged or belittled. Boundaries.

I don't like people touching my hair without asking. Boundaries.

I ask guests to remove their shoes before entering my home. You have a problem with that, don't come over. Boundaries.

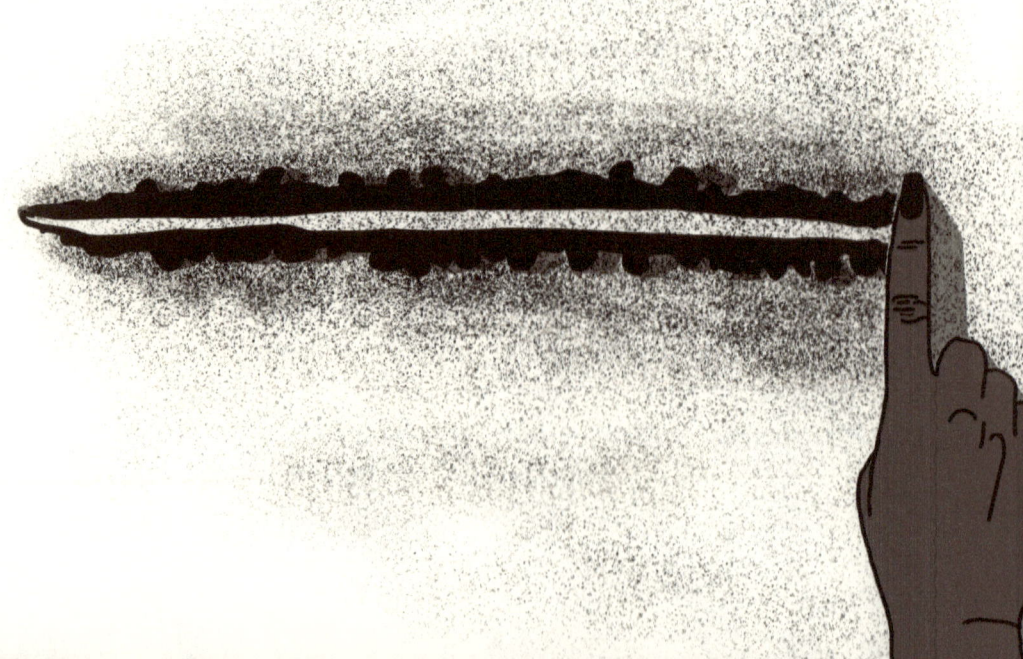

I am not comfortable with my two-year-old son driving with any-one but me and his father, unless absolutely necessary. Boundaries.

I don't like to talk about money. Boundaries.

I am open to suggestions, but don't tell me how to raise my child. Boundaries.

I don't allow just anyone to hold my son. Boundaries.

I don't like unexpected guests. Don't show up at our home without an invitation. You don't know what we have going on. Boundaries.

I think it is rude to overstay your welcome. Boundaries.

I have a few others, and I'm sure the list will get longer as my children grow.

I can see your face. I can feel you judging me. But as I get older, I'm begin-ning to recognize that as a woman and a mother, I will not always be understood, but if you say you love me, you'll accept my boundaries.

> You don't have to like it, but you do have to respect it.

HOW HONEST ARE PARENTS?

I don't feel my twins are ugly, but I do pray they have a great sense of humor.

My family gets so frustrated when I say things like this, but in my heart of hearts, my seven-week-old twin boys are "interesting" looking. The Lion, the oldest by sixty seconds, is *huge*. He looks like a middle-aged undisputed champion sumo wrestler who fell behind in his taxes. And Lord don't get me started on my Little Old Man. His face could really use a smile. He looks like that grumpy grandfather who lived on the corner and cursed the kids for walking on his grass.

I'm just being honest. As a matter of fact, if more parents were honest about their children, the world would be a better place. My husband is a schoolteacher, and every evening he comes home and tells me about the troubled student he teaches. Instead of the parents appreciating the fact that a teacher cares enough to correct their child, they actually come up to the school irate that someone would chastise their precious angel. Come on! You can't tell me that these parents don't know that their son or daughter is a full-blown jerk. And they are well aware that the way their child acts at home is the way they act in the classroom, but instead of being honest and saying, "My child is an asshole," they would rather be in denial.

I remember being in the fifth grade and I came home and told my mother that Anthony Thomas shouted that I was "two pieces of bread that wished I had some meat." When I threatened to tell the teacher, he called me "Channel 11" because to him I was just two skinny legs. I was so embarrassed. I went to my mother for comfort, and do you know what she did? She laughed. Do you know why she laughed? Because it was funny!

Of course, after her laughter subsided, she gave me a hug and told me that I was beautiful, but she also went on to explain to me that I was skinny and I would probably be that way for a long time, so the best thing for me to do was embrace it. My mother was honest, and her honesty helped me to build character. My mother also told me that Anthony probably liked me. Boys are such idiots!

As parents, we love our children, but if your child has a big head, don't act like it's small. If your child bites through furniture at home, don't act surprised if the teacher calls and says your child was put out for biting a child. If your child is sensitive about being cross-eyed with buck teeth, address the obvious at home, and help them develop a stand-up routine, quick! Bottom line: Let's be honest about our children.

I was reading a book by one of my favorite authors, Dan Brown, and the story's main character said something that struck me: "The human mind has a primitive ego defense mechanism that negates all realities that produce too much stress for the brain to handle. It's called denial."

I would rather build on a foundation of strong character than on a weak lie.

HOME FOR THE HOLIDAYS

It has been a long f@#king week! Oh yeah, you better cover your ears because it's about to get diaper-rash raw in this joint.

Traveling to see both sets of families during the holidays (long-distance) with two infants and a toddler is enough to make any reasonable parent curse.

S. Dot (the two-year-old) has unlimited energy, and his favorite word is "No!" Amir, the younger, more menacing-looking twin, was in a fussy mood because his twin brother was sick and therefore received more attention. Now Nas wasn't your average sick baby—a few coughs and the sniffles. He was literally projectile vomiting every bottle he drank. And when he wasn't drinking a bottle, he would throw up whatever liquid his stomach could produce. It reached the point that we stopped putting clothes on him, stripped him down to his diaper, ditched the cute burping cloths, and wrapped him like a burrito in an oversized luxury beach towel. Did I mention it was "luxury"?

It was a madhouse, I tell you! Between washing and folding clothes every three hours, running back and forth to the doctor's office, rolling around on the floor trying to entertain S. Dot and balancing crying babies while vomit dripped down my bra, my husband and I did not have a moment to breathe. So, excuse my language if I dreaded the thought of traveling to our families' homes for the holidays.

Do you know how tedious it is to pack for two newborns and a toddler (who isn't potty trained)? I'm talking diaper bags, strollers, boppy pillows, rock and plays, bottles, bottle warmers, booster seats, snacks, DVDs, toys, medicine, pacifiers, bibs, a back-up change of clothes, a back-up to the back-up change of clothes, camera, phone charger, and the dishes you were asked to make for dinner? You add all of this to the weight of carrying two huge-ass infant car seats, and I guarantee you that it will be difficult to find kind words when you are finally driving to your destination with a Honda Pilot full of screaming babies and you have to make a U-turn because you forgot your gotdamn cell phone—which, by the way, you left on the kitchen table next to your gotdamn wallet!

Of course nursery school was closed last week, so we had a full house. And no matter how much people say, "Just let us know how we can help," no one was trying to come over and watch our three children.

Man, I remember when the holidays used to mean a few days of relaxation, but when a couple decides to have children, every day is a workday and there is no rest for the weary.

Are we there yet?

PARTY OF FIVE

Maybe it's because I was raised in Sandtown-Winchester, a historically oppressed community in Baltimore constantly marred by bias and stereotypes. After Reagan coined the phrase "welfare queen," a Black woman with multiple children became a dog whistle in America to play on racial anxieties. I grew up knowing that people believed that Black women had a bunch of children so they could beat the system and force taxpayers to take care of them.

When I found out we were going to be a family of five, I just knew I would be viewed as ghetto when people saw three toddler boys trailing behind me as we traveled throughout the city.

I know I sound ridiculous, but the sense of embarrassment I felt was real. I thought I was pregnant with our second child, not twins! What can I say? Sometimes the foolishness we hear from our past still haunts our present.

Granted, I am blessed to have a hardworking husband, and we pride ourselves on taking care of our family, but the idea of raising more than two children is a hard pill for me to swallow. Sometimes I feel like I need to wear a shirt that says, *I didn't ask for three kids, God just decided to super-size me.*

I remember calling my girlfriend in hysterics.

> **Me:** I'll never be able to take them to an amusement park. Five is an odd number, and I don't want one of my boys sitting next to a stranger.
>
> **Friend:** *<side eye>*

Me: I prefer booth seating in restaurants. A family of five can't sit in a booth—not without one parent being on double duty. Then their food will get cold.

Friend: *<shaking head> <side eye>*

Me: These car seats are so damn big we will be forced to trade-in. I'm too fly for a minivan.

Friend: *<rolling her eyes>*

Me: And who the hell wants to babysit three children overnight?!? These kids are the flesh of my flesh, and half the time I don't even want to watch them.

Friend: *<hangs up the phone>*

Okay, maybe I'm overreacting. I know I am not the first person in the world to have more than two children, as one friend loves to remind me.

Her: Girl, back in the day, our great-grandparents and great-great-grandparents had ten, twelve, and fifteen children.

Me: Um, our great-great-grandparents didn't have all of those children out of love—it was a necessity. They needed help picking cotton and harvesting sugarcane in the blazing sun. I, on the other hand, am a modern-day woman with a salary. I don't need help in the fields, though I wouldn't mind a tax write-off.

Her: *<hangs up the phone>*

I have two arms and three children; don't judge me if it freaks me out.

HELLO, MY NAME IS

I was in the ninth grade when Shakespeare hit me with "What's in a name? That which we call a rose / By any other name would smell as sweet."

Obviously, Shakespeare didn't know that Bonkeisha Jenkins and Hensessy Brown may find it challenging to land a corporate job because of the bias against "Black" names . . . or names white people are not familiar with.

It's a general understanding within the African American community. And I resent it.

So, when the time arrived to select names for our sons, "we did it for the culture."

Jason and I are proud eighties babies. We were raised in the era of slouch socks, nineties R&B music, and Motorola pagers. We wanted our sons' names to tell a story that marked our period in time.

Hip-hop changed the world just as we know our sons will.

Before I continue, I need you to understand that my husband is not "a fan" of Jay-Z. Even to suggest that word would be egregious. Jason is a philosopher and scholar of Jay-Z's life through lyrics. He is what you would call a HOV connoisseur. Needless to say, it didn't take us long to decide to name our firstborn son, Shawn, after Mr. S. Dot Carter himself, "the greatest rapper of all time" (to quote my husband).

Now, despite the ease of choosing Shawn's first name, it took divine inspiration to decide on his middle name.

One night, I was taking a shower, and I remember thinking to myself, "We need a middle name. I don't know what it is. But whatever we call him, it has to be big! I'm talking BIG-BIG!"

I nearly slipped on the black soap when it hit me. "Biggie, Notorious BIG, Biggie Smalls—THAT'S THE NAME! THAT'S THE NAME!"

No, Shawn's middle name is not Notorious BIG. It's Christopher after hip-hop legend Christopher Wallace.

We were so pumped. Plus, we had the added bonus of sticking it to the system. With a name like Shawn Christopher, it is hard to discriminate. A person can't readily assume who is walking through the door.

Two years later, when we discovered we were having two more babies, I was so scared and overwhelmed by the thought of being a mother to twins that I wasn't very excited or in a rush to name them. Subconsciously, I knew that this would require me to accept my new reality. I was going to be a mother of three boys whether I felt I was ready or not.

It was late in my second trimester when I started to open up and connect with my twins. I was beginning to feel their personalities and energy. They were distinctly different, even in the womb. They seemed to be perfect polar opposites, like yin and yang.

One of my favorite Jay-Z lines is "You was who you was before you got here." Well, you could say the same about our twins.

Now, for the aficionado, it is well known that the relationship between Jay-Z and his longtime friend, Emory Jones, is a real-life depiction of "my brother's keeper." And it was in that spirit of love that we named Twin A Emery. We wanted him to be a support for his brothers.

We were planning to name Twin B Carter, as a nod to Jay-Z's last name, but we didn't want to be corny.

Twin B felt like a force of nature. When he would move, I would get lightheaded and dizzy, like the earth was spinning off of its axis. My husband wanted a strong name to match Twin B's strength, so we called him Liam, which to me sounded like the kind of name a girl would like to brag to her girlfriends about. But Liam still did not have a hip-hop link like his brothers, and his name didn't rhyme with his twin, which was a deal breaker for me.

It was during brunch that my girlfriend and line sister, Proctor, looked at me from across the table and said, "If you gonna name your children after Jay-Z, then it is only right that one of them boy's names is Nasir."

Proctor and I met in high school, and like my husband, she is also a connoisseur, but the number 1 on her top 5 list is Nas Escobar (aka Nasir bin Olu Dara Jones). Bar for bar, beat for beat, when you ask Proctor, "Ain't nobody coming for God's Son."

I thought about it, and the competitive lyricism between Nas and Jay-Z will forever go down in history as one of the greatest hip-hop music clashes of all time. Plus, there was something about the way Liam moved inside the womb that told me that Nasir would be a perfect middle name for him.

Considering that Nasir is Arabic for "protector, supporter, and helper," we wanted Emery's middle name to be similar to his twin brother.

Unlike Liam, who was a stone boulder laying on my pelvic bone, Emery was constantly stirring and causing me severe heartburn and vomiting throughout my entire pregnancy. He just couldn't keep still. It was as if he was running in place, like the Energizer Bunny turned on his side. During ultrasounds, Liam would either be really chill or sleep, while Emery excitedly bounced and took center stage.

We chose Amir for Emery's middle name, which is Arabic for "prince and ruler." It was also inspired by one of the most prolific musicians and record producers of the twenty-first century, QuestLove (aka Ahmir Khalib Thompson).

I love to tell the story of how we came up with our sons' names because I agree with Shakespeare, a rose is just a rose, and a name is just a name. But I believe that this cannot be true when you understand the manner and intention by which the rose and the name were given.

It's not the name. It's the meaning behind it.

THE KEY DIFFERENCE BETWEEN BOYS

I always said that if I had children, I only wanted boys, and boy was God listening!

Now as I look at my three sons and try to imagine what their futures hold, I realize the one flaw of not having a daughter. I will never experience the joy of helping my daughter find her fairy-tale dress for her storybook wedding. I will not be my daughter's first call after she feels my grandchild move in her womb for the first time. These are intimate moments that are traditionally shared between a mother and her daughter. It has now hit me that when my sons find the woman they choose to spend the rest of their lives with, I will become the mother-in-law. Even the title sounds cold. *Mother-in-law.* The "in-law" basically reinforces that your rights as a mother are limited.

Granted, if the mother-in-law has a fair relationship with her son's future wife, she may still be included in these monumental occasions, but don't get it twisted: she will have to play second fiddle to her daughter-in-law's mother. And who are we fooling? After you have spent nine grueling months carrying your son, sixteen excruciating hours in labor with your son, eighteen tumultuous years raising your son, and seven years on your knees praying that God covers your son as he ventures out into this wild world on his own . . . by the time your son is twenty-five years old, you are not jumping at the chance to see him rush down the aisle or become someone's "baby father" after being in a relationship for only a few months.

I am starting to realize that it's not that mothers aren't willing to give another woman a chance with their son, it is that there is no woman on earth who will have spent more time loving your son than you have. And sometimes, that can be a difficult pill for "protective mothers" like me to swallow. Wow, I'm starting to get a headache. I called my girlfriend who is also a mother of boys and I shared my revelation. She responded, "Um, before we worry about our son's future wife, let's focus on which brand of diapers to buy and what pre-school we're going to send them to?"

I hope my son's future wife is an orphan.

HOW DOES YOUR CHILD SEE YOU?

I am a severely flawed human being. Actually, depending on what day you catch me, you might not even consider me a human being. But Lord knows I'm trying.

If you told me ten years ago that one day I would be married with three children under three, two of which are twins, there's a good chance I would have kicked you in the balls (whether you had balls or not).

My husband and I will tell you, "Having three babies is hard!" When I'm not working a full-time job, my home life is filled with washing clothes, making bottles, cooking, changing diapers, wrestling on the floor, tickle fights, reading children's books, toilet training, singing songs, negotiating food consumption (i.e., "If you finish eating your green beans, Mommy and Daddy will give you ice cream after dinner"), watching Nick Jr., Disney Jr., and Sprout, blowing bubbles, giving baths, suctioning noses, kissing boo-boos, deciphering incoherent toddler babble, washing dishes, sweeping the floor, dumping the trash, wiping tears, and picking boogies—all in no particular order. But I'm not complaining. I get it. As parents, we do what we have to do, right? No one congratulates you at the end of the night.

There's no parade or fireworks with your name blazed across the sky and a crowd chanting, "Job well done!" or "It couldn't be done without you!"

Honestly, if I can get sixty seconds to sit on the toilet without a random toddler busting in the door singing "Itsy Bitsy Spider" or asking to play *Wallykazam* on my iPad, I'd say that is a reward in and of itself!

Yet, in the midst of this whirlwind we call parenthood, I don't think it's unusual for a parent to wonder, *Do my children see me, I mean REALLY see me?!?* Well, this Mother's Day, I received my answer.

Last week S. Dot's daycare provider, Ms. Marsha, had all of the children look through piles of magazines to find a picture of their mother to cut out and paste on cards. She told me that my two-and-a-half-year-old son sat at the table for a long time flipping through dozens of magazines. He didn't rush the decision so he could carry on with playtime. She tried to help him, pointing out Black women, white women, short, tall, etc., but S. Dot kept saying "No, that is not my mommy." After a good amount of time had passed, S. Dot walked over to the teacher, holding a magazine and exclaimed, "Ms. Marsha, THAT'S my mommy!"

So, they proceeded to cut and paste the woman's photograph on a card. On Sunday, my two-and-a-half-year-old son presented me with flowers he personally selected and a card that represented the woman *he* perceives *me* to be.

The woman was natural, beautiful, and stylish—with a hint of attitude. In a nutshell, she was everything I would love to think I am. For my two-year-old son to compare me to her, I was beyond moved. I cried. My heart felt full. In that moment, I realized that a man's first perception of a woman is through his mother.

Yes, I'm far from perfect, and I have made my share of mistakes, but when I saw myself through my son's eyes, it made me stand a little taller, hold my head a little higher, and work a little harder. And isn't that what it's all about?

> The children are watching. Try to give them something worth seeing.

THE CONSTANT VS. THE VARIABLE

Which One Are You?

I have a weekly call with my grandparents who live down south. Recently, my grandmother went on and on about how much she would love for my brother to call her. She told me how she prays and thinks of him often. She swooned about how she loves hearing his deep voice say, "Hi, Grand-MAW." She reminisced how my brother loved eating peanut butter and jelly sandwiches as a child. Gag me with a jagged spork! As I held the phone away from my ear, rolling my eyes, I could feel my blood boil up my back.

Here's the deal: I take the time to check on my grandparents, make sure they are okay rumbling around in their double-wide trailer home —on bricks. My grandmother would kill me if I didn't note that the trailer has a brick build-in. Anyway, I take the time to check on my grandparents, and all I get are questions about my younger sibling.

When I was thirteen years old, my nine-year-old brother said something to me that I will never forget: "Dionne, you're too good, and now that's all people expect from you. But look at me, I do just enough, which makes anything extra I do exciting." No truer words have ever been spoken by a nine-year-old.

It's literally the story of my life. My husband described this situation perfectly. He calls it the "the Constant vs. the Variable." I'm horrible at math, but the principle is simple: The *constant* is the element that remains the same. The *variable* is the characteristic or element that always changes.

As a mother, sister, friend, wife, employee, I have seen the "the Constant vs. the Variable" equation at every level.

My best girlfriend, let's call her Andria because that's her real name. She hated all of my other aliases for her. Dria often shares her story as an example of my theory. She felt that her brother was rushing entirely too fast into his relationship with a young lady he had only known for a couple of months.

Just to give you some background: Her younger brother and his "girlfriend" (an older mother of two) had both ended long-term relationships and now, after three months of dating, were planning to marry. It was a rough adjustment for the close-knit family, a lot of heated arguments, hurtful words, miscommunication, and silent treatment. It's odd how sometimes love can make people act so ugly. Because Andria is the oldest and has often been viewed as the most responsible, it put her in the middle of drama. She tried to be a voice of reason. It was devastating to see her parents hurt by her brother's changed behavior.

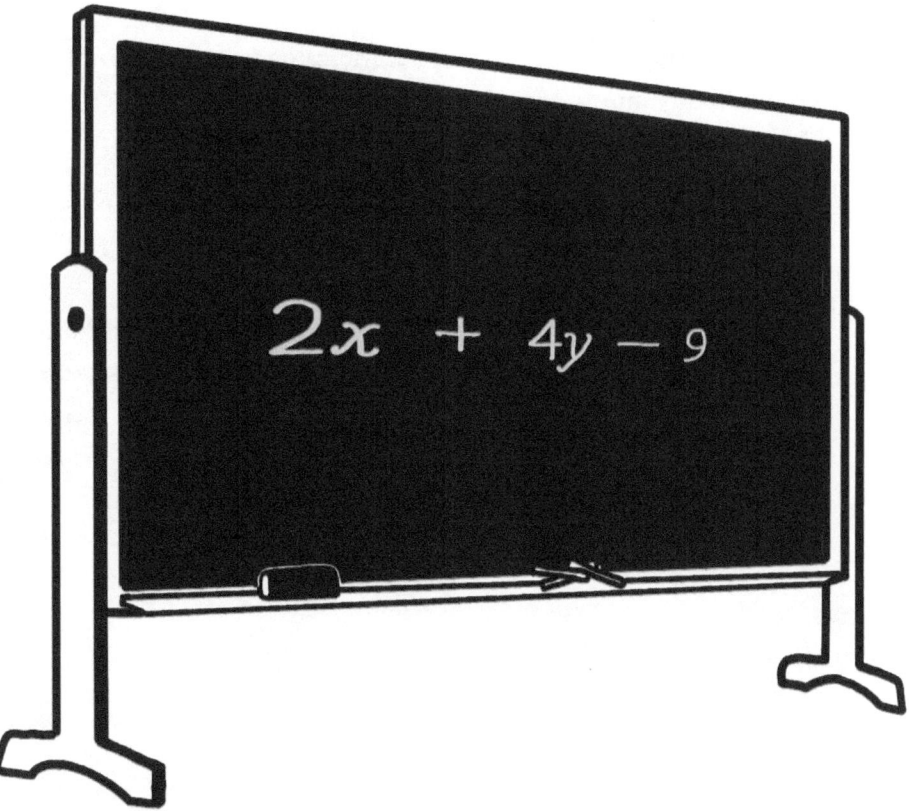

My apologies, let me get to the point.

Andria's brother marries, and of course her new sister-in-law feels resentment toward the family. Not too long after marriage, her brother and his wife have a son, and they allow very little (if any) involvement from the family. The son doesn't visit his parents or remember birthdays or anniversaries. Dria witnesses her parents' efforts to try to get in her brother's good graces despite the way they were personally treated. They constantly send cards and gifts to her brother and his wife, with the hope of making amends. On the opposite side, Dria is a pleaser and often feels overlooked.

It's not ironic that Andria and I have been friends since sixth grade. We are both Type A overachievers who are fueled by the acknowledgment that we have our shit together—or at least loosely packaged. We strive to do well, and we want to do well by the people around us, but time after time we feel taken for granted. After yet another weekly vent session with Dria, my husband poured me a glass of wine and told me, "Babe, y'all need to stop putting the cherry on top, especially if you are expecting a round of applause!"

Damn, I wasn't sure if it was the pink Moscato, or if my husband had just blown my mind.

He was right. People like me and Andria need to check our priorities. Are we doing what we are doing because it is right or because it is expected? Are we doing what we are doing because it's what we want to do or because we want to be acknowledged? Are we giving our best or just enough to be noticed? If it is the latter, then we lost before we started.

> The constant remains unchanged, therefore allowing time to focus on the variable. Everyone plays their role.

FALL AND RISE AGAIN

I was watching the BET Awards last night with my husband. He's a stand-up comedian, so to hear his commentary and live tweets is quite hilarious to me. When Sean "Puffy" Combs took the stage and the Bad Boy logo filled our flat-screen, we—just like every other eighties baby couple we knew—felt a wave of excitement and then the realization: "Wait, it's been twenty years?! How old are we?"

Reminiscent of being under my parents' roof, I danced around the living room well aware that if one more classic song dropped, we were going to wake the entire neighborhood. And now that we're the parents of three little boys, the consequences are dire—but man, it felt so good. Then, for a split second, out of nowhere, I saw Puffy drop from the bottom of the screen, then pop back up as if he were doing a split. I asked my husband, "Did you see that?" "See what?" he asked as he steadily typed out a tweet.

"Did Puffy fall?" I asked. But before the last word left my lips, Diddy was at the front of the stage leading the crowd in the chant, "I thought I told you that we won't stop! I thought I told you that we won't stop!" It was as if nothing had happened.

Of course, after the performance, which left me sweaty from my poor rendition of the Harlem shake, I saw that social media was all abuzz with Puffy's fall. The memes were rolling in.

Don't get me wrong, I live with a comedian, I have a sense of humor. But Puffy's split-second tumble was a reminder of the times we are living in.

I want my sons to understand that as they grow and chase their dreams, there will be people who will watch from the side and laugh at their missteps, relish when they fall, look forward to their tumbles. There will be people who will take more joy in pointing out everything that went wrong rather than praising everything that went right. I need my sons to understand the magnitude of allowing these people to distract or deter them from doing what they love.

I know you are probably thinking, *Dionne, it was just an award show performance. It's not that deep.* But I see lessons in everything. I respect the fact that Diddy kept moving with the same or maybe even more energy than before he fell. That's the mark of a true showman. And while the memes populated our Instagram and Twitter feeds, Diddy received a huge-ass check from BET, rode in the back of his huge-ass escalade, which dropped him off at his huge-ass penthouse, and he and his personal assistant had a huge-ass laugh at all of the jokes from the people who were and will always be spectators.

> It's hard to hear the people on the sidelines when you're too busy playing the game.

COSMETIC SURGERY

Sign Me Up?

Mommy Magician: Gather round, children. Would you like to see a magic trick?

<magician sticks fist through the middle of her stomach>

Children: Eww, yuck! How did you do that?

Mommy Magician: It's called diastasis recti.

Children: What does that mean?

Mommy Magicians: It means that when you little bastards were born, you split your mother's abdominal muscles, and her stomach has never looked right since!

If God gave women the blessing of childbirth, then the devil is responsible for her body's recovery.

I have always been small-framed. If it wasn't for a decent chest, I'd look like a teenage boy.

After college, I was between 120 to 130 pounds. After marriage and my first son, I weighed around 140 pounds. When I was pregnant with my twins, I skyrocketed to 205 pounds. <record scratch> I repeat: 205 pounds!

My body wasn't prepared to take on the additional weight. My skin began to split and blister.

Have you ever seen a drowning victim? Well, that would have been my closest comparison. The preeclampsia caused me to swell in ways unimaginable. I was forced to wear my husband's sneakers because no shoe in my closet fit. My son would squeeze my legs so he could see his handprint in my skin. When I walked, I could feel the fluid move across the top of my feet. By the end of my pregnancy, I was miserable. I looked like something you would find tangled in a fisherman's net.

My mother was in awe that I was carrying twin boys. She would quote Chaka Khan: "D, you are every woman! Be proud." What she really meant was, "You look like you swallowed every woman."

I prayed that I would shed the pounds quickly, as I had done with my previous pregnancy, but I wasn't ready for what was to come. On October 11, 2013, the day my twins were born, I weighed 200 pounds, and by November 11, 2013, I was down to 125 pounds. Everyone was excited and shocked by how small I was. They thought I looked great, but they hadn't seen me naked.

Most people do not understand the effects of dramatic weight gain and loss. When you push and stretch your body beyond the weight it's used to in a short amount of time, and then quickly drop the pounds, it doesn't know how to react. And the results are always most visible when you step out of the shower and see yourself in the mirror under fluorescent bathroom lighting. (Grab a towel quick and run!)

Have you ever baked a chocolate cake and it falls, and the top is *really* dark, wrinkly, and loose? Yeah, that's how my stomach looks. The hole in the middle of the cake is the equivalent of my stretched navel. I used to have a cute belly button, but now it looks like a droopy eyelid. And let's not talk about my chest. I have a serious attitude with my breasts. I refuse to even give them eye contact. I talk to them as if they

can respond.

Me: You two look ridiculous! This is the best you can do? Y'all get on my nerves. Look at you, just lying there! Where's your initiative? Sit up straight. Stop slouching! For the love of God, DO SOMETHING!

I never thought I would ever consider cosmetic surgery, but how is it cosmetic if I am simply asking the doctor to do what I tell my toddler all the time: "Put things back the way you found them"? Hell, I'm not trying to look nineteen again, but I don't see anything wrong with wanting to look the way I did nine months before I sacrificed my body to give life to two babies at the same damn time.

My girlfriend believes that women should embrace their natural bodies because the body is our temple and God made everyone unique. And the fact that a woman would consider having surgery is shameful, vain, and irresponsible.

Don't get me wrong: I understand where she is coming from, but in no way am I racing out the door to get injections in my ass so I can have a behind larger than Nicki Minaj, nor am I asking for huge silicone implants so I can have breasts the size of hot air balloons. If there aren't enough crunches and push-ups on God's green earth to remove the excess skin on my stomach and lift my breasts, then I believe I'm entitled to take the money God gave me and reclaim my "temple."

If I had da money, there'd be no loose skin on my tummy!

SIX WAYS HAVING A DOG DOES NOT COMPARE TO RAISING CHILDREN

Today, I found myself sitting in a meeting surrounded by new dog owners. I listened as they gushed over their pups. The conversations swirled around me: "I told my son he's gonna have to walk him." "The dog plopped on our bed at four o'clock in the morning." "I went to pick up the poop and realized I forgot the bag." They cherished their new responsibilities. Then, it happened. One of the dog owners exclaimed, "Well, I guess we know what it's like to have children!"

<record scratch>

Seriously?! The casualness with which animal owners without children compare their lives to those of people raising a child is getting out of control. Even if you say, "Well, I know it's not *exactly* the same. I'm just saying I can relate." No, you can't. You know why? Because parents have the whole "parenting thing" on lock. It's an exclusive club. And if you're confused about membership, below are six distinct ways having a dog is *nothing* like raising a child.

NUMBER SIX

It's a *FREAKING* dog!

NUMBER FIVE

The flexibility of easily leaving your house alone goes out the window once you have children. I can't leave my sons in a cage for six hours while I go to work. Well, I could, but I would be writing this from my jail cell.

NUMBER FOUR

Related to number five, people are quicker to watch your pet than your children. I was speaking to a father of three who told me that he and his wife were planning a trip to Jamaica. His neighbor was quick to offer to watch his dog and feed their bird. Even his mother-in-law called and said the pup could stay with her. She would enjoy the company. His response: "I'm not concerned about someone watching these pets. I need someone to watch these kids!"

NUMBER THREE

It is reported that the cost of raising a child until the age of eighteen is roughly $300,000. That's per child—in a TWO-PARENT household. Yeah, I'm just gonna leave this right here.

NUMBER TWO

Dog owners can go online and do their research before venturing to a dog rescue to find the breed that matches their lifestyle. Guess what? No amount of research prepares you for carrying a baby for nine months. Hell, the second time around, I carried two babies at the same time. In the end, a baby does not arrive in a dog carrier wearing a bow around his collar. My new little addition was delivered through a very small opening in my nether regions.

NUMBER ONE

As a dog owner, do you get on your knees at night and pray that God protects your animal? Do you ask God for the strength you need to raise him to live to his full potential and make a lasting contribution to his society? Do you pray that your dog meets someone who will love and cherish him long after you're gone? Do you lose sleep due to the worry and the sacrifices you've made?

Well?!

I'll wait.

Before you label me Cruella, please know that I am a dog lover, and I value the joy animals bring to a person's life. But enough is enough with the comparisons.

You are barking up the wrong tree.

FEELING SOME KINDA WAY

Childbirth is ironic, isn't it? A mother carries life for nine months, the effects on her body are astounding, and the pain of delivery is excruciating. Yet, when a mother loses her child, the pain felt during birth is eclipsed by the unfathomable torment of her child's life being snatched.

On February 26, 2012, Trayvon Martin was killed. He was a seventeen-year-old African American boy who was fatally shot by a neighborhood watch volunteer in Florida. My firstborn had just turned six months old.

On July 17, 2014, Eric Garner died in New York City, after a police officer put him in a choke hold for fifteen seconds. Three weeks later, on August 9, 2014, Michael Brown was killed. He was an eighteen-year-old African American boy who was fatally shot by a police officer in Ferguson, Missouri. During it all, my firstborn son was preparing to turn three years old, and I was pregnant with twin boys.

On my birthday, April 4, 2015, Walter Scott, an African American man, was killed after a South Carolina police officer shot him eight times in the back. Two weeks later, on April 19, 2015, Freddie Gray died of a severe spinal cord injury after Baltimore City police arrested him.

My stomach turns as I recall the stories and see the news footage. In my head, I repeat the words "There but for the grace of God go I." These men were husbands, fathers, brothers, . . . sons. Sons. They were once infants. Each one was carried by a woman in her womb for nine months, only for that woman to later watch them killed. The horror. I weep. I weep as a mother of three beautiful Black boys. I weep for my husband, who leaves out the door every morning with the very real thought that his life could be taken.

There are moments when you just want to get away. But on June 17, 2015, two days after taking the boys to South Carolina for the first time to visit with their great-grandparents, nine people were killed by a gunman at the Emanuel African Methodist Episcopal Church in Charleston. My world seemed to be spinning out of control, and before I could catch my breath, one month later, on July 13, 2015, Sandra Bland, an African American woman, was found dead in a jail cell in Waller County, Texas. She was arrested for failure to signal a lane change. News surfaced as my husband and I were planning my son's fourth birthday party, just a few days after our twins turned a year and a half.

It feels unreal. There are moments throughout my day that I am dizzy with despair. It's hard to focus or channel the anxiety.

I was driving home last week, listening to a comedy station on Pandora, and I heard Louis C.K.'s bit on the food chain:

> It must be awful to be other stuff. I'm glad I'm this [pointing at himself]. This is a pretty good deal considering the alternatives . . . anything else, any other kind of thing and you're in the food chain, YOU ARE IN THE FOOD CHAIN! We're out of the food chain. I don't know if we fully appreciate the fact that we got out of the food chain—that is a massive upgrade, because for every other living thing, life ends by being eaten . . . That's how all life ends. That's every single life except human life. Every life ends like this, "Ahhh, ahhhh—AHHHHH!" We're the only ones that get to just die old in a bed like, "I love you, bye."

Immediately, I burst out laughing, which then faded to one of those soft, closed-mouth chuckles. You know that sound you make when you've come face-to-face with irony. As a mother of three little boys, I can't help but feel like it's open season on Black lives, and we're at the bottom of the food chain. Of course, that's not what Louis C.K. is referencing. He's talking about lions chasing down wildebeests and spiders trapping flies, but at that moment I felt a strong connection.

I've sat up nights wringing my hands with my head hung low, weighed down by fear. How can I protect my sons, my husband, my family . . . myself? But that's when I lean on faith and love. Believe me, I don't wear rose-colored glasses, but I do know that I can't change a negative situation with bad feelings. Yes, evil exists, and it would be a disservice to my children if I did not make them aware of the darkness in this world, but as my father taught me, "When faced with evil doings, you can either allow it to make you bitter or better." I choose the latter. If not for myself, then for all those lives lost.

> Hope is being able to see that there is
> light despite all of the darkness.
>
> —Desmond Tutu

BLACK-ISH

A Black Mother's View

When the show *Black-ish* first premiered, I received text message after text message from friends saying, "Girl, this show is all about you and Jason!" (Jason is my husband's name.)

At its core, *Black-ish* follows a modern-day, middle-class African American family. The parents have reached a perceived level of success, and they live in a world where cultural assimilation has caused Dre (the father) to try to create a sense of ethnic identity for the members of his family that will allow them to honor their background while preparing them to embrace the future. Of course, this leads to numerous episodes of hilarious awkwardness and challenges to stereotypes.

Sometimes, I feel like *Black-ish* is taking pages from my life. I grew up on the west side of Baltimore. My earliest memories are from Sandtown-Winchester Apartments. I remember there being more dirt than grass, and no matter how clean my mother kept our house, the roaches were still familiar guests. The one car we had stayed on cement blocks, so we walked or took the bus everywhere. That is why I walk so fast now. The worst thing a child can do is lag behind a Black mother. I wore a house key around my neck from the age of eight, and I was responsible for taking care of my little brother and cousins, some of whom were older than me. My family was made up of God-fearing fighters, hustlers, deacons and pastors, and people who may not have had college but they were self-taught geniuses who used what they had to provide for those they loved. With that as my foundation and a mother who stressed the importance of education, I grew up having street and book smarts. Fast-forward thirty years later.

My four-year-old has never taken public transportation, and when he gets into a car, he expects that his iPad and Nabi are fully charged and that an organic apple, pea, and spinach pouch is on chill in my purse. He's never been to a corner store because we live in subdivision full of cul-de-sacs. When I take my son back to where I grew up, the difference is striking. S. Dot is mild-mannered, and the thought of fighting drives him to tears. As a mother, growing up as I did, I am often scared that my son is not "hard" enough. Last night my husband and I had a conversation, and it went something like this:

Me: I just want S. Dot to be able to handle himself. I'm not saying he has to be hood. I just want him to be aware that the streets exist.

Him: You know he's four, right? Babe, we are his parents. We are here to teach him and guide him. He will learn from us and our experiences. At the end of the day, I'm more concerned with our son having good credit than street credit.

Me: I know. I know. But you've seen those sheltered children. I want S. Dot to be well-rounded. I am shaped by where I'm from.

Him: Dionne, you can keep it real without roaches. Go to sleep!

And there you have it. At the end of the day, when it comes to raising a family, and especially as a Black mother raising three Black boys, I've learned to focus on surrounding my children with people with their best interests in mind and offering varied life experiences. It takes a village for a reason, people!

Granted, you may still encounter comical situations, like your son getting into your friend's car for the first time and saying, "Mommy where's the TV?!" but that just becomes another teaching moment.

> There are three rules for raising a well-rounded child. Exposure. Exposure. Exposure.

CATERPILLAR CATERPILLAR

I haven't been in a positive place for a few months, and it is affecting my spirit. There is so much darkness spreading throughout the world it has been difficult for me to find a balance between my "surrounding reality" and my "immediate reality." What does that mean? Well, my surrounding reality includes the growing protests of the Black Lives Matter movement, and my city is still reeling from Baltimore's uprising over the death of Freddie Gray. Or how about the 129 deaths in the recent Paris attack, or the 147 deaths at Garissa University in Kenya?

These are just a few of the things in my "surrounding reality." But my immediate reality is that my twin sons have a speech delay, and we are stressing trying to figure out how much our insurance will cover the treatment. All of these are important challenges to solve, but only one depends on my immediate attention.

Lately, my "surrounding reality" has started to weigh on me. It's hard for me to put my boys to sleep while holding back tears recounting the last moments of Kendal Fenwick's life. A twenty-four-year-old father of three who I didn't even know. While French fries and chicken nuggets warmed on the stove for his family, he stepped out to his car and was gunned down. He was an activist who cared about his community and wanted better for those around him. He stood up to the drug dealers in his neighborhood, and he paid the ultimate price.

What creeps into my mind during the few quiet moments I have during the day is that police officers say that, as Kendal was being fired upon, he ran away from his home rather than toward it to protect his family. His children were his last thoughts.

That's what my husband would have done. That's what my father would have done. My uncle, my brother, my father-in-law . . . they all could be Kendal Fenwick.

This shit is scary.

My husband and I had to move from a home we loved because we constantly had run-ins with ignorant neighbors and dealers who would sit on our steps or the hood of our cars. They would blast loud music, curse, and throw trash. My husband and I would confront them and call the police. And yes, they would leave for a moment, but they always returned. There were others in the neighborhood who were just as frustrated, but they were older and scared of confrontation. My husband, being the man he is, was never willing to back down. And after a while, we became known for being outspoken. Because of this, our house and our cars were vandalized, and there were days we felt like hostages in our own home. Then we found out we were pregnant with twins. I was honestly faced with the fact that, one day, one of these confrontations was going to turn violent and I could lose my husband . . . either by death or jail. I would be left to raise three boys on my own. All of this was because we wanted a safe environment for our family. We ultimately moved.

Kendal Fenwick did not. He was a lone wolf among monsters.

In no way am I saying that Black people are not disproportionately targeted by the police in America. But I am also saying that the streets have a longer reach than the law. And because of that, it is sometimes easier to fight against the political system than it is the gang right outside your front door. And if you don't believe me, ask the relatives of the Dawson family and countless others across the country who stood up and said, "Not on my watch."

I may not have the answers now, but S. Dot, Amir, and Nas are fanning a fire in me that I can no longer contain. Thanks to my babies, I am growing braver and stronger with every new life experience they encounter. Not every day is a good one. And I don't doubt that worse can't come. But motherhood is like the bedtime story I tell the boys, *The Very Hungry Caterpillar*.

Over the last five years, I have been responsible for not only one life but three whole human beings. THREE OF THEM.

I've screamed, I've cried, I've doubted, I've cursed—a lot. I've felt out of control, I've felt lost and lonely, but, because I am a mother, I've

had to get up. As Nipsey says, "It's a marathon."

I love my sons to the moon and back and to infinity and beyond. I want my three princes to one day reign as kings. And to make this happen, my boys are challenging me to be the change I want to see.

Each morning, I'm waking up like the caterpillar—exhausted—but with renewed purpose and an awareness that I am so much bigger than I give my body credit.

Just when the caterpillar thought the world was over.

EPILOGUE

You Owe Me an Apology

I was born and raised in the most "human" city in America. I'm a Baltimore girl through and through. My cell phone number still starts with 410.

I was the firstborn grandchild, showered with love but weighted with responsibility. I was what the church folks called an "old soul." Immaturity wasn't a luxury afforded to me. I was a young Black girl maneuvering the streets of Sandtown-Winchester, seventy-two square blocks of layered history.

In the eighties, my grandfather would love to boast of Baltimore's most notable figures. I sang to Billie Holiday. I wanted to be as intelligent as Thurgood Marshall. And I loved to listen to my mother recite Langston Hughes' "Simple Stories" on the radio.

But to this day, if I had to rank my all-time favorite superheroes, they would be:

Harriet Tubman

Storm

Okoye

And this is why I feel we are doing a disservice to our youth.

Despite a litany of examples displaying the power of African Americans, I was still constantly cautioned by those who loved me the most that my best would never be good enough. It became my expectation that I would be required to work ten times harder than my white counterparts and receive ten times less.

Now, as an adult, I wish I could say they were lying. But a 2016 survey by the Federal Reserve found a 10-to-1 difference in the median wealth/net worth of white and Black Americans.

As a young Black woman, it became my expectation that my feelings would be regarded less than my white counterparts' feelings, so I must remain friendly, steady my anger, watch my face, and adjust my tone so as not to scare, offend, or intimidate.

Now, as an adult, I wish I could say they were lying. But in 2018, six-time US Open tennis champion Serena Williams received what she felt was an unfair penalty from the referee. Naturally, she was frustrated, a reaction not uncommonly seen by male players. And yet, the bizarre escalation was a reaction far too common to racially conscious women who are intentional about the things they say and advocate for, aka Strong Black Women.

I can still hear Serena shouting at the referee, "You owe me an apology! You owe me an apology! I have never cheated in my life. I have a daughter, and I stand for what is right for her, and I've never cheated. You owe me an apology!"

I cried.

God knows, I cried . . . hard.

I felt the daggers of anger wielded through her words. My mouth watered as my body flushed with heat. I was in fight-or-flight mode.

It was then that the paradigm shifted. I closed my eyes, and I began to see chairs slowly disappear from a table. A table that all my life I had been told symbolized power, credibility, and success.

I heard the voices of those who loved me most, and I realized that their teachings, though well intended, were preventing me from understanding my worth. And as a mother raising three Black boys in America, I would forever owe them an apology if I didn't become my own superhero.

I underestimated your value, your power, and your influence. I made you believe that you deserved to work harder and receive less. I left you to fight in the most toxic environments and mask it as "strength." I caused you to doubt your intelligence and your ability to impact change.

I apologize for holding you back, Dionne.

Girl, you will NEVER lose your seat at the table because YOU ARE THE TABLE!

I'm a bad mother—

ABOUT
DIONNE JOYNER-WEEMS

Dionne Joyner-Weems is a natural-born storyteller who hails from the west side of Baltimore. She and her husband are proud Morgan State University graduates, and they are raising their three dynamic sons a stone's throw away from their alma mater. Dionne is known as a CEO mommy with a colorful energy that is authentic and unparalleled.

www.ingramcontent.com/pod-product-compliance
Lightning Source LLC
Chambersburg PA
CBHW030313130626
46549CB00002B/831